Online Group Activities to Enhance Counselor Education
J. Scott Glass & Kylie P. Dotson-Blake

ASGW

Association for Specialists in Group Work

Others in the ASGW Group Activity Book Series (available at www.asgw.org)

Group Work Experts Share their Favorite Activities: A Guide to Choosing, Planning, Conducting, and Processing

School Counselors Share their Favorite Activities: A Guide to Choosing, Planning, Conducting, and Processing

Group Work Experts Share their Favorite Multicultural Activities: A Guide to Choosing, Planning, Conducting, and Processing

Brand New:

Printable Handout Companion Guides for All Three Books

CEUs for All Books and DVDS

Mood Smiley Face Stress Balls, Question Balls, and Magic Wands

Dvds also available from ASGW:

Developmental Aspects of Group Counseling (Stockton)

Group Work: Leading in the Here and Now (Carroll)

Leading Groups with Adolescents   (DeLucia-Waack, Segrist, & Horne)

Group Counseling with Children: A Multicultural Approach (Bauman & Steen)

Group Counseling with Adolescents: A Multicultural Approach (Bauman & Steen)

Published by
Association for Specialists in Group Work
5999 Stevenson Ave.
Alexandria, VA 22304

ISBN 9781-55620-338-1

Dedication

To my wife, Bonnie, and my children, Katie and Sam, the best small group ever.

- Scott

To my husband, Mitchell, and my sons, Kaden and Xander—I am honored to be a member of our group!

– Kylie

Table of Contents

Activities for Multicultural Counseling (and More)

Activities for Group Counseling (and More)

Activities for Legal & Ethical Issues in Counseling (and More)

Activities for Clinical Experiences (and More)

Activities for Assessment & Research Methods (and More)

Activities for Human Development (and More)

Activities for Helping Relationships (and More)

About the Editors

J. Scott Glass is an Associate Professor in the Counselor Education program at East Carolina University. Prior to his appointment at ECU, he taught at Elon University and Mississippi State University at Meridian. Dr. Glass received his Bachelor's degree from North Carolina State University, and attended East Carolina University for his Master's degree in Counselor Education. He then earned his PhD in Counseling and Counselor Education from the University of North Carolina at Greensboro. As a Licensed Professional Counselor (North Carolina) and Nationally Certified Counselor, Dr. Glass has worked primarily in an outdoor setting where adventure based programming was offered. These programs emphasize group work and aim to foster group cohesion while focusing on group dynamics, problem-solving and processing.

Dr. Glass' areas of interest include adventure based counseling, group work with all ages, processing, and issues related to diversity in counseling. He has served as President of the North Carolina ASGW, and served on the editorial board for the *Journal for Specialists in Group Work* for over 10 years. He has had numerous presentations at the international, national, and state levels on topics related to adventure based counseling and group work.

Kylie P. Dotson–Blake is an Assistant Professor in the Counselor Education program at East Carolina University. Prior to her appointment at ECU, she taught as a visiting professor at the College of William & Mary. Dr. Dotson-Blake received her Bachelor's degree and Master's degree from East Carolina University before attending the College of William & Mary for her PhD in Counselor Education. As a Licensed Professional Counselor (North Carolina) and Nationally Certified Counselor, Dr. Dotson-Blake has worked primarily in the areas of family counseling and school counseling.

Dr. Dotson-Blake's areas of interest include family counseling, school counseling, sexual identity, family-school-community partnerships, and diversity issues related to counseling. She has served as President of the North Carolina ASGW, and currently serves on the Board of Directors for the National Board for Certified Counselors. She has had numerous presentations at the international, national, and state levels on topics related to family counseling and culturally-inclusive family-school-community partnerships.

FOREWARD

J. Scott Glass and Kylie P. Dotson-Blake

Given the success of ASGW's previous activity books, and the fact that more and more Counselor Education courses are being taught (at least in part) via an online format, we decided that creating a book aimed at online activities for counselor educators would be useful. As the field of education continues to change as technology is being infused into classrooms at an amazing rate, we thought it would be helpful to compile a number of activities that counselor educators could implement in their courses.

Each activity stands alone and includes goals and learning objectives, suggested courses for usage, a point in the group when activity might be best implemented, estimated time length, technology needs, directions for the activity, processing questions, possible adaptations, and potential cautions or issues that might arise. In addition, three introductory chapters are included that we hope will help counselor educators examine issues related to online group work, building a sense of community via online education, and group dynamics that may take place. While the activities are organized by suggested courses for their usage, we encourage all readers to read them through a creative lens, and (like all effective group counselors) imagine how they might be adapted for use in other courses or with other topics as well.

We greatly appreciate the efforts of those who contributed activities to this book and hope that you will enjoy using them and find them helpful in promoting effective learning communities in your online counselor education courses.

Chapter 1

Teaching Online and Online Group Work

in Counselor Education

J. Scott Glass and Kylie P. Dotson-Blake

The teaching landscape is continuously evolving to meet the demands of engaged, contemporary learners. As access to the Internet and online tools has increased, so has the integration of such technologies in the field of education. Traditional brick-and-mortar buildings are no longer the only educational learning environments available to students. Students are participating daily in pre-service and professional development training programs from the comfort of their own homes and offices via the Internet. Historically, effective teaching has taken place inside the walls of a classroom as teachers and learners interacted and delved into the material. Today those same courses are being adapted to virtual platforms. As online learning advances, more collegiate-level courses are being delivered in online environments (Krieger & Stockton, 2004). No longer are institutions of higher learning bound by classroom walls, or limited by the necessity of specific, inflexible class meeting times. Educational settings are increasingly turning to online education to supplement, enhance or even replace traditional teaching approaches (Alavi & Leidner, 2001; Palloff & Pratt, 2001).

The Association of Public and Land-grant Universities (APLU) Sloan National Commission on Online Learning reported that in 2008-2009, 33% of more than 10,000 faculty members surveyed in a benchmark study of online learning had taught an online course and 25% were currently teaching an online course (Allen & Seaman, 2010). With the increased prevalence of online courses being offered in higher education in the years spanning 2008-2012 (Allen & Seaman, 2011), one could infer that the percentage of faculty currently teaching online courses would be even higher at this point. Additionally, just as online courses have increased in the last five years, so has the availability of online tools and new technologies.

These new technologies may forever change the look and experience of higher education while providing increased access to educational services for students (Hollenbeck, Zinkhan, & French, 2005). However, making the switch from traditional teaching models to online education is not simply a matter of repackaging content. It takes a great deal of effort and planning to effectively teach online courses and it requires the instructor to explore and utilize a range of technology and tools. Faculty participating in the

APLU Sloan report (Allen & Seaman, 2010) also asserted that preparation for online courses is more intense than that of traditional face-to-face courses and that fewer resources were available to assist faculty with this preparation. The critical task for faculty using such new tools is to create and share lessons of high quality that students can embrace and teachers can maintain (Dykman & Davis, 2008). The need for increased attention to course preparation and support in the development of high quality online courses for counselor education is at the core of the intent of this text.

It is critical that counselor educators are well-prepared to engage with students in a variety of ways. Still, while there are numerous important differences between teaching in a traditional classroom and teaching via online education, there are similar goals that have not changed, regardless of the modality used. For example, effective teaching requires clear expectations and directions and meaningful experiences designed to enhance learning, relationships and cohesion among students (and with the instructor). Counselor education requires students to reflect on personal values and perspectives and to share those with classmates. Sharing personal information with others requires trust and cohesion within the group. Online counselor education classes are no different and building this trust and cohesion demands that the counselor educator design activities such as video introductions and blog discussions that allow students to get to know each other, build relationships and develop trust in each other.

An easy example of a way to start building these relationships and fostering cohesion is by requiring students to prepare and post a brief video introduction and then requiring that all students view and comment on the video posts from their colleagues. By opening the class with student video introductions, students are able to begin the process of getting to know each other and develop relationships. They are able to make connections that extend beyond online discussions of course content. One student in an online class shared with the authors that her favorite part of the opening video introductions is observing the homes and spaces where her classmates choose to make their videos. She said, "I just feel like I get a sense of the whole person through our video intros. I get to see the dogs and children running by while my colleagues try to tape their intro or I get to see their office space with rows of books or well-organized desks. I just get a sense of who the person is and what they value, right from the first brief introduction in our online class." We believe supporting students in their efforts to engage in their online courses in a genuine, open manner is central to fostering strong relationships and effective group cohesion.

In all Counselor Education classes, relationships must be encouraged and student learning and growth within the discipline must take place for teaching to truly be effective. Instructors need to facilitate learning in an interactive environment, allowing students to learn the material while engaging in substantive learning experiences with instructors and classmates. Though many goals of learning do not change between methods of class offerings, the ways instructors teach typically require some adaptation. Abbott (2005) explained that teaching well online is vastly different from teaching in a brick-and-mortar classroom.

Online Learning

The Internet has become a common medium for instruction across the globe. This technology allows for the development of unique learning opportunities allowing students and instructors to interact and communicate in innovative ways. The role of the teacher and the nature of teaching, is changing as more online programs and courses are being offered and more faculty are being asked to engage in online teaching (Bennett & Lockyer, 2004). The change from traditional methods of instruction to various forms of distance education instruction present numerous challenges for instructors. Palloff and Pratt (2005) break these challenges into four primary areas: a. Participation Challenges, b. Leadership and Decision-Making Challenges, c. Course and Activity Design Challenges and d. Cultural Differences Challenges. These challenges hold particular impacts for fostering group cohesion and facilitating processing within group counseling and classroom Counselor Education experiences. These challenges and potential resolutions are discussed in more detail below.

In the area of participation challenges, instructors must establish clear expectations for student participation and engagement at the beginning of every online course and must strive throughout the course to clarify these expectations and gauge students' understanding of such. Instructors must monitor levels of engagement and make determinations about optimal levels, modifying course processes as appropriate. For example, if instructors realize during a class that the sheer volume of discussion threads or posts means that some elements of course content are being lost in the tidal wave of information, then it may be necessary to modify the expectations for student posts. Think about a classroom where every student is asked to shout out five distinct ideas about a particular aspect of course content, it would be quite chaotic and it would be possible that in all of the student responses, we lost the opportunity for actual student reflection. Participation challenges are often discussed by online instructors as a question of how to increase participation, but it may be just as true that an instructor has plenty of participation from students and that the question then is how to enhance the QUALITY of that participation rather than increase the quantity. The challenge of participation requires online instructors to be continually monitoring the class and responding flexibly to the needs of the particular group of students.

Leadership and decision-making challenges are another source of challenges that requires ongoing instructor evaluation and flexible response. Instructors in face-to-face courses are able to work collaboratively with students to make determinations about changes in course processes, deadlines, and content as necessary for the appropriate progression of the course. This need not be different in an online course. Instructors who are actively engaged with students and who encourage high quality, consistent student engagement are able to also make decisions about course changes and processes collaboratively with students. Being flexible and developing a process of working collaboratively with students for decision-making can position the instructor as a strong leader of a course that evolves to meet the developmental needs of students.

Course and activity design challenges are the primary focus for this text, though the other areas of challenge will be discussed and addressed as appropriate. Addressing the challenge of course and activity design successfully will allow the instructor to fulfill a primary requirement of effective online courses as posited by Palloff and Pratt (2005), "to reduce isolation and maximize learning potential by creating social presence" (p. 36). Integrating activities into one's course that are developed to intentionally build community and foster cohesion enables the instructor to craft a context ideal for reflecting, processing and growing. Some of the challenges faced by instructors in the area of course and activity design include the following:

- Well-designed activities that are not clearly connected to the course content or the focus for the lesson in which they are embedded.
- Activities that lack substance, that are focused on "doing" but do not include opportunities to process what was learned and what it means for the student as a professional. This happens often in online classes where the activity itself becomes the focus and there not a forum or plan for processing.
- Activities that are increase the isolation of the students, rather than more firmly connecting the classroom community.

All of these challenges can be addressed by the instructor with intentional planning and thoughtful attention to the development and support of the classroom community. The activities presented in this text are designed to assist Counselor Educators with their efforts to integrate meaningful activities with clear plans for processing into their online courses.

Cultural differences challenges encompass cultural differences in communication styles, disclosure and perceptions of the appropriateness of disclosure, perceptions of time management and allocation of tasks and responsibilities. These differences can be surmounted through careful attention to building relationships, clarifying expectations and requirements and ongoing perception-checking with students by the instructor. The onus of responsibility for creating an environment in which cultural differences are respected and strong working relationships are built lies with the instructor with a need to be thoroughly engaged in collaborative relationships with students.

The literature demonstrates that there are positive and negative sides of the debate regarding the efficacy and appropriateness of online learning in various areas of academia (McCracken, 2002). Simply changing lecture notes into text and sharing information via email or instant messaging is not enough to ensure quality learning experiences and the development of content mastery. In order to address these changes effectively, teachers at higher education institutions must rethink their cultural, academic, organizational, and pedagogical structures of teaching and learning (Howell, Saba, Lindsay, & Williams, 2004).

Given that studies have shown higher levels of learning are not easily achieved in online courses (Kreber & Kanuka, 2006), instructors must rethink how material is shared, how students interact, and how to facilitate learning in online environments. Often teachers have little or no experience teaching online, and therefore attempt to transfer traditional teaching approaches to the online classroom (Baran, Correia, & Thompson, 2011). The literature supports the notion that online teaching is not the same as face-to-face instruction, therefore requiring the development of its own pedagogies (Kreber & Kanuka, 2006; Laat, Lally, Lipponen, & Simons, 2007). Content of material and roles of teachers can be transferred to the online environment, but not without some adaptation to new roles in order to create meaningful learning experiences (McShane, 2004). It would be irresponsible, and most likely ineffective, for instructors to simply continue engaging in exactly the same pedagogies as they make the transition into a virtual learning environment. Online learning inevitably changes the way responsibilities in the classroom are performed (Baren, et al, 2011).

Roles of Online Instructors

The roles of online instructors are many. Research has identified a number of main roles of online teachers including content expert, instructional designer, materials producer (Aydin, 2005), facilitator, advisor/counselor, assessor, content facilitator, designer, manager/administrator (Goodyear et al., 2001) and professional (Bawane & Spector, 2009). It can be overwhelming for instructors to wear so many hats, while at the same time trying to learn new modalities, technologies and platforms. Online course delivery is often difficult, perhaps especially for first-time users, because instructors are unclear how to effectively take lessons or activities that have previously been effective in a face-to-face classroom setting, and adequately transition them to an online environment. The difficulty does not only remain in the actual adaptation of the activity, but in the quest to make sure the activity retains the same high quality effectiveness in the online classroom that the instructor previously was able to facilitate in the face-to-face classroom setting. At the core of effective instruction in Counselor Education is the teacher-student relationship. This is one aspect that remains constant for both face-to-face and online courses. As online instructors perform the many varied roles and responsibilities required of them, content expert, instructional designer, facilitator, etc., he or she must constantly ask himself/herself, "Is my work in this area strengthening my relationship with students and the relationships among students in my classroom community or does it result in increased isolation of participants in our community?" Though some tasks within any classroom are going to be conducted individually, it is important that most enhance the connectedness and cohesiveness within the community in order to maximize the learning opportunities.

Counselor Education

In Counselor Education, as in most higher education disciplines, more courses are being offered as fully online or as campus-based with an additional online component. As the number of students participating in online courses in Counselor Education programs increase, the importance of providing effective instruction that focuses on the needs of those graduate students is critical. To meet the needs of these students, counselor educators must be prepared to access and utilize available technology. The literature on online learning emphasizes the need to create learning environments where dialogue and interactions (both student to student and student to instructor) can be the benchmark of a good education (Ekong, 2006; Garrison, Anderson, & Archer, 2001). In a program such as Counselor Education, where there is such a heavy emphasis on the development of relationships, it is important that instructors are able to facilitate these bonds even as the curriculum is being shifted to an online format.

There are a number of positive indicators that point to reasons Counselor Education programs might want to include some distance education courses. To begin, many universities view this medium as a way to help offset the shrinking classroom (Altekruse & Brew, 2000), which provides the institution a means of generating revenue and staying relevant in a competitive marketplace (Anakwe, Kessler & Christensen, 1999). Given the changing marketplace and economic uncertainties, it is important for institutions of higher learning that they remain utilized and relevant. In addition, simply the convenience of attending class from home and having the ability to work at times most convenient to the student adds to the interest in this type of learning. Perhaps most convincingly is that some researchers suggest that students engaged in distance learning environments learn in 70% less time than their counterparts who are in a traditional classroom (Parlangeli, Marchigiani, & Bagnara, 1999). One explanation may be that discussions and processing of content and ideas are no longer limited by class times. Instead, interactions may be ongoing and activities come with more time to process and reflect. Supporting this supposition, Hara, Bonk and Angeli (2000) asserted that giving the students additional time to process activities via distance education resulted in student contributions that involved greater levels of cognition.

While there are advantages to distance learning, it would be misleading to suggest that it does not present some perceived disadvantages. Some challenges surrounding distance education include difficulty using software (including software upgrades), ease for students to cheat, student self-motivation given that deadlines are often flexible, limits to home computers and testing difficulties (Altekruse & Brew, 2000). In addition to these items, some students may also struggle with the availability of the instructor. Given that the class may not have identified meeting times, as with face-to-face courses, students may become frustrated at the lack of clear times when the instructor may be contacted. These challenges, however, can be addressed by Counselor Education programs and faculty that intentionally plan online courses that build in transparent and clearly communicated expectations and meaningful opportunities for students to connect with each other and the faculty member teaching them.

Rogers (1951) believed that that genuineness, empathy, and unconditional positive regard were critical in regards to positive outcomes in counseling. In addition, it has been suggested that the relationship between the counselor and the client is a crucial component related to positive outcomes in therapy (Bordin, 1994). The question then becomes, can counselor educators teach these skills to counselors-in-training via an online format?

There are several concerns that are typically present when Counselor Education programs consider using the Internet to offer courses. One such concern is whether or not "techniques" courses can be as effective when taught online in contrast to a face-to-face class. There is debate about which courses might, or might not be, appropriate for distance education. It is likely that some programs offer courses entirely online while others offer courses in a hybrid mode (mix between online and meeting in a traditional classroom). As more programs move towards using more web-based technologies to enhance learning, it is critical that counselor educators learn to create learning environments within the virtual classroom.

Ascough (2002) went so far as to label the medium of distance education as cold. Is it reasonable then, to think that this type of helping professional training can occur in a virtual learning environment and foster student learning? Often students and instructors communicate through the use of text-based programs, such as emails or instant messaging systems, so students may not as easily be able to pick up on some of the skills typically modeled by instructors they observe in a face-to-face classroom. Most people can speak to a time when the receiver perceived the tone of an email or text message as rude or hostile when the sender did not intend for such perceptions. Considering these experiences, can online instruction truly be used to train counseling professionals when the nuances of emotion, expression and fostering relationships are absolutely imperative for effective professional training that promotes the development of strong counseling skills and identities for students?

It is the belief of the editors of this text that online instruction can certainly be used to facilitate the professional development of counselors. However, the editors also hold the belief that effective online instruction in counselor education requires intentional, thoughtful preparation of courses that are infused with activities promoting self-reflection, group engagement and a process of building a learning community. By integrating effective activities into online courses, counselor educators can create learning experiences that both meet the needs of contemporary students while also honoring and addressing the need to help pre-service counselors develop and understand empathy, genuineness and the other skills crucial for counselors.

An important part of creating effective online learning environments is making sure that course activities are value laden (DuCharme-Hansen & Dupin-Bryant, 2005). Therefore, the task for counselor educators is to develop effective activities or assignments that not only help students learn course content, but also provide support for the learning community in order to promote students' professional development in an online setting. The hope is that counselor educators are able to create such activities, but it can be overwhelming to develop such experiences for the widely divergent courses required as part of the Counselor Education curriculum and this text is intended to serve as a resource to help professionals with this facet of course preparation.

The profession acknowledges that it is a key function of counseling to help clients reflect on their actions, ways in which they think, personal responses, and decisions (Cormier & Nurius, 2003). Similarly, it is important for counselor educators to create opportunities for this level of reflection in classes, regardless of whether those courses are taught online or face-to-face. Traditionally, experiential activities and opportunities for guided reflection, skills practice and self-assessment have been deemed critical for effective learning in the field of counselor education (Ancis, 1998). Unfortunately, the paucity of resources relevant to transferring these activities from their typical use in face-to-face classroom settings to online learning environments leaves educators struggling to create connected, effective learning communities in their online courses. Subsequently, these courses may be delivered primarily in a lecture format without the benefit of interactive activities to promote student learning and development which can then be transferred into professional practice as helping clients engage in reflection to promote growth. Having a toolkit that includes experiential activities for online Counselor Education professional development would help to infuse these online learning communities with the traditional spirit of "learn, engage, reflect and counsel" that has been such a strong foundational building block for the profession of counseling.

Ethical Issues in Online Learning

Online education has experienced incredible growth in the past 10 years (Anderson & Simpson, 2007), and while this growth has brought about new technologies and perhaps greater access to learning environments, it also brings with it unique ethical concerns. As more instructors begin teaching online for the first time, it is important that these instructors are prepared for potential challenges they may face. Teachers who have been successful educators in face-to-face classrooms must recognize that transitioning to an online format is more than simply moving materials to a web-based platform. Copying handouts and notes to the internet does not ensure that students will engage with classmates and instructors, or learn content at similar rates. Any faculty who teaches online must ask himself or herself, "What is the key to helping my students learn?" and then seek to incorporate these critical factors into the online learning experience. Many educators would answer this question with assertions of the importance of student engagement, a supportive, active learning community, ongoing assessment and feedback by the faculty. The authors of this text agree and would also add that all teaching, online or face-to-face requires a high level of intentionality on the part of the educator. It is critical that the instructor carefully plan how material is delivered, how students interact, and what activities are used in order to maximize learning. Additionally, instructors must seek to continually engage in self-evaluation of the learning experience, identifying challenges and concerns and modifying the experience as necessary to promote the growth of students.

One ethical issue raised by the use of online instruction relates to equality and equity. Brey (2006) asked, "Does a reliance on computer networks in higher education foster equality and equity for students and does it promote diversity, or does it disadvantage social classes and force conformity?" (p. 91). Often, the perception of online education is that it gives greater access to learning, however Simpson (2005) stated that so far there is little evidence suggesting that this type of medium will overcome social exclusion or increase participation in education. The idea is that those who typically feel disadvantaged in our educational system will continue to experience similar disadvantages when faced with online learning (Anderson & Simpson, 2007). It is likely that, given the access to and availability of technology at many universities, educators incorrectly assume that all learners have access to the internet, thereby making e-learning easy and convenient for all. The cost of equipment (i.e., computers, webcams, internet access) alone may prohibit many from participating in this type of learning environment, not to mention the potential need of students to be trained in how to use the internet and web-based learning platforms.

Another area of potential ethical concern to which online instructors must attend is that of multicultural issues in the online environment. Certainly the issue of valuing diversity is a topic that counselor educators should be emphasizing throughout a program's curriculum. While students are required to take a course on multicultural issues, consideration of culture and diversity is most likely (and certainly should be) discussed and woven into the content of every other counseling course as well. Such an emphasis would surely not change for online courses, yet instructors must recognize that teaching online may change the concerns related to how this is monitored. For example, in a face-to-face class when there is a discussion between students related to diversity, the instructor is there to facilitate and immediately address problems that may arise as a result of the conversation. With online discussions, there is certainly potential for miscommunication among students brought on by cultural differences (Goodfellow & Hewling, 2005), and the instructor is not always immediately present to facilitate and resolve sudden conflicts. Another concern lies in unaddressed concerns and perceptions. In a face-to-face class, instructors are able to attend to body language, facial expressions and the level with which students are engaged in class discussions. From this information, the instructor can make efforts to draw students into the conversations, respond to concerns that may not be verbally expressed and direct conversations to topics that might only be minimally touched upon without the added information raising the instructor's awareness of the need for further discussion. In an online learning experience, some students who feel uncomfortable or who disagree with the majority may choose to simply not respond or participate. Without efforts on the part of the instructor to determine factors behind non-participation or efforts to broaden the discussion to invite a wider range of viewpoints on the part of the students, topics could stay at a more surface level rather than having the instructor identify concerns, provide information and opportunities for meaningful interactions and allowing the class to grow together.

In addition to the topic of diversity being an issue in need of monitoring, the diversity and culture of the individuals participating in online learning will have an impact on how it is delivered. The importance of cultural differences in relation to how students communicate and interact has been acknowledged (Collis & Remmers, 1997). The question for instructors then becomes how do they encourage and monitor participation in online discussion in a fair and equitable manner when communication styles and interaction may be, at least in part, influenced by cultural systems? Goodfellow and Hewling (2005) suggest that students who do not fully engage in the class discussions and activities diminish the classroom community's ability to learn collaboratively. It is important for online learners to recognize their responsibility to their classmates and teachers, as well as to themselves (Haughey, 2007). Furthermore, it is imperative that online instructors provide activities and assignments that are structured in such a way as to promote the students' awareness of the responsibility they have to their classmates.

When teaching in a face-to-face class, instructors often think about the presence that they bring to the learning environment. This type of presence has been described as opening up to others in a dialogical way (Starratt, 2004). Because this has historically been done through verbal exchanges and physical presence, it is clear that online education presents unique challenges where this is concerned. Ethical issues could arise as a result of online participants pretending genuine presence or refusing to meet expectations of a committed presence (Haughey, 2007). Certainly an online instructor, as is true of any instructor, should lead a class by example. If a teacher wants to promote fairness, responsibility and genuineness, then it is reasonable to expect this person to interact with students in a manner that promotes these concepts. Just as a client/counselor relationship may be strengthened by genuine self-disclosure on the part of the counselor, so can the relationships in the classroom be enhanced in a similar manner. Perhaps the key is for the instructor to set the course up in a way that encourages these types of values and behaviors. The teacher should openly share her expectation of fairness and genuineness. It should not be assumed that these types of qualities will simply happen as a result of being in a class. It is essential that instructors provide activities and craft opportunities for meaningful interactions between students in online learning communities. By implementing such activities, instructors create for themselves opportunities to observe students, get to know them and thus be able to gauge the sincerity and genuineness with which students present. Then, this information can be used to guide students as they reflect on their experiences, interactions and professional development. Instructors must be intentional in how they create the learning environment in order to experience the benefits of genuine exchanges and confidentiality among students.

Perhaps the ethical issue garnering the most attention is the possibility of dishonesty among students in online learning. Sileo and Sileo (2008) suggest that the additional time and energy required to complete extra assignments, loneliness and absence of personal interaction with classmates and professors may encourage cheating on the part of participants. It is not a surprise that the popularity and growth of the Internet has brought about numerous opportunities for dishonesty to occur. There are websites that allow those interested to purchase papers to use for required assignments (Fain & Bates, 2001). Furthermore, it is possible for students engage in conversation with classmates during online examinations (Sileo & Sileo, 2008) or look up answers and distribute to peers (Olt, 2002). While cheating has historically been a concern of instructors, online learning certainly presents unique challenges and considerations not experienced in the traditional classroom. Fortunately, in many universities and colleges, resources assist to help instructors become aware of how to identify cheating and how to prevent and address it.

Because of the aforementioned concerns, it is important that instructors strive to develop online classes that deal proactively with these issues. Many structural elements can be crafted to address these concerns, including clarity of expectations within the syllabus, stated parameters for using outside resources and support to develop assignments, etc. For example, teachers need to be clear regarding their expectations regarding classwork, assignments and examinations. If the instructor believes that working collaboratively on a particular assignment is cheating, while it is deemed acceptable on a separate assignment, these differences and directions should be made clear to students. It is possible that this level of scrutiny is seen as overwhelming to instructors, especially those teaching online for the first time, however this attention to detail could potentially avoid uncomfortable situations down the road if dealt with early in the class.

Developing Effective Classes: The Importance of Community

A primary concern that emerges in a review of the pedagogical and ethical challenges of online learning is the concern of the isolated learner. Ethical behavior is easier to facilitate and connections between learners and between the learners and instructor are more likely in a course where students feel invested in the learning community and responsible to each other. Traditional definitions of community (e.g., Hillery, 1955) were typically based on geography, referring to a group of people living in a particular place, along with the idea that "community" included the interaction among members sharing a common purpose and an awareness of these commonalities (Moisey, Neu, & Cleveland-Innes, 2008). However, in today's world of email, Internet, blogs, Wikis, texting and Facebook, our understanding of communities has changed and is continually evolving. Communities now may consist of people from a wide variety of geographical regions and areas of the world, connected by various modes of technology. The introduction of the Internet has given rise to the notion of virtual or online communities, and the concept of "communities of practice" (Moisey, Neu, & Cleveland-Innes, 2008). Wenger, McDermott and Snyder (2002) suggested that "communities of practice are groups of people who share a concern, a set of problems, or a passion about a topic, and who deepen their knowledge and expertise in this area by interacting on an ongoing basis" (p. 4).

The development of an online community of practice" is considered an integral part of web-based learning (Moisey et al., 2008). In addition, sense of community is one variable seen as a potential mediator in the retention of students in online education (Carr, 2000; Rovai & Wighting, 2005). When students feel connected and engaged in their learning community, they are more likely to be invested in the community and less likely to withdraw from the learning experience (Palloff & Pratt, 2005). This concept of community is not new, and learning environments that foster interaction and social learning have been identified as being a critical feature of higher education for decades, well before the Internet and online courses were introduced (Drouin & Vartanian, 2010).

The process of developing strong, connected, cohesive learning communities is imperative for online counselor education courses and online activities in group counseling to be successful. This text seeks to share activities to facilitate the process of online learning in counselor education and the coming chapters will focus on how to effectively foster group cohesion and support the emergence of connected learning communities. Though online learning experiences are different in many ways from traditional, face-to-face learning experiences, the importance of connectedness and community are consistent across both.

In closing, it is imperative that instructors fully consider the potential impact of embedding group activities in online learning experiences. By encouraging group work, instructors have the opportunity to foster cohesiveness and a strong learning community while also supporting students' connections to other students in the program. Building these networks of support can truly help students get the most out of their counselor education program and can also promote the retention of students who might otherwise be likely to isolate themselves from others in their classes. Online group activities present some ethical concerns, but for the most part, these concerns can be addressed by carefully planning one's course to promote honesty, openness and a willingness to engage with others in respectful and trustworthy ways by all students. Clearly communicating expectations, using available resources and careful monitoring on the part of the instructor can further help to minimize ethical dilemmas. Most importantly, group activities in online courses provide the instructor with a highly valuable benefit, the benefit of getting to know each student better as an individual and as a professional. This knowledge and familiarity can help instructors gauge the academic progress and professional development of students, which is an absolutely essential component of preparing professional counselors.

References

Abbott, L. (2005). The nature of authentic professional development during curriculum-based telecomputing. *Journal of Research on Technology in Education, 37* (4), 379-398.

Alavi, M., & Leidner, D. E. (2001). Research commentary: Technology-mediated learning—A call for greater depth and breadth of research. *Information Systems Research, 12* (1) 1-10. http://dx.doi.org/10.1287/isre.12.1.1.9720

Allen, I. E., & Seaman, J. (2011). *Going the Distance: Online Education in the United States, 2011.* Newburyport, MA: Babson Survey Research Group and The Sloan Consortium.

Allen, I. E., & Seaman, J. (2010). *Learning on Demand: Online Education in the United States, 2009.* Newburyport, MA: Babson Survey Research Group and The Sloan Consortium.

Altekruse, M. K., & Brew, L. (2000). Using the web for distance learning. In Bloom, J. W., & Walz, G. R. (Eds). *Cybercounseling and cyberlearning: Strategies and resources for the millennium* (pp. 129-141). Greensboro, NC: American Counseling Association and ERIC/CASS.

Anakwe, U. P., Kessler, E. H., & Christensen, E. W. (1999). Distance learning and cultural diversity: Potential users' perspective. *International Journal of Organizational Analysis, 7* (3), 224-243. http://dx.doi.org/10.1108/eb028901

Ancis, J. R. (1998). Cultural competency training at a distance: Challenges and strategies. *Journal of Counseling & Development, 76*(2), 134-143. http://dx.doi.org/10.1002/j.1556-6676.1998.tb02386.x

Anderson, B., & Simpson, M. (2007). Ethical issues in online education. *Open Learning, 22* (2), 129-138. http://dx.doi.org/10.1080/02680510701306673

Ascough, R. S. (2002). Designing for online distance education: Putting pedagogy before technology. *Theology and Religion, 5,* 1, 17-29. http://dx.doi.org/10.1111/1467-9647.00114

Aydin, C. (2005). Turkish mentors' perception of roles, competencies, and resources for online teaching. Turkish Online Journal of Distance Education, 6, 3, Retrieved on January 27, 2012 from https://tojde.anadolu.edu.tr/tojde19/index.htm

Baran, E., Correia, A., & Thompson, A. (2011). Transforming online teaching practice: Critical analysis of the literature on the roles and competencies of online teachers. *Distance Education, 32*(3), 421-439. http://dx.doi.org/10.1080/01587919.2011.610293

Bawane, J., & Spector, J. (2009). Prioritization of online instructor roles: Implications for competency-based teacher education programs. Distance Education, 30(3), 383-397. http://dx.doi.org/10.1080/01587910903236536

Bennett, S., & Lockyer, L. (2004). Becoming an online teacher: Adapting to a changed environment for teaching and learning in higher education. Educational Media International, 41(3), 231-248. http://dx.doi.org/10.1080/09523980410001680842

Bordin, E. S. (1994). Theory and research in the therapeutic working alliance: New directions. In O. A. Horvath & L. S. Greenberg (Eds.), *The working alliance: Theory research and practice* (pp 13-37). New York: Wiley.

Brey, P. (2006). Social and ethical dimensions of computer-mediated education. *Journal of Information, Communication and Ethics in Society, 4*(2), 91-101. http://dx.doi.org/10.1108/14779960680000284

Collis, B., & Remmers, E. (1997). The world wide web in education: Issues related to cross-cultural communication and interaction. In B. Khan (Ed)., *Web–based instruction.* Englewood Cliffs, NJ: Educational Technology Publications.

Cormier, S. J., & Nurius, P. S. (2003). *Interviewing and change strategies for helpers* (5th ed.). Pacific Grove, CA: Brooks/Cole.

DuCharme-Hansen, B. A., & Dupin-Bryant, P. A. (2005). Distance education plans: Course planning for online adult learners. *Tech Trends: Linking Research & Practice to Improve Learning, 49*, 31-39.

Dykman, C. A., & Davis, C. K. (2008). Online education forum: Part two – teaching online versus teaching conventionally. *Journal of Information Systems Education, 19* (2), 157-164.

Ekong, J. I. (2006). What factors facilitate online counselor training? Experiences of campus Alberta graduate students. *Journal of Distance Education, 21*(1) 1-14.

Fain, M, & Bates, P. (2001). Cheating 101: Paper mills and you. Retrieved February 3, 2012 from http://www.coastal.edu/library/presentations/papermil.html

Garrison, D., Anderson, T., & Archer, W. (2001). Critical thinking, cognitive presence, and computer conferencing in distance education. *American Journal of Distance Education, 15*, 7-23. http://dx.doi.org/10.1080/08923640109527071

Goodfellow, R., & Hewling, A. (2005). Reconceptualising culture in virtual environments: From an 'essentialist' to a 'negotiated' perspective. *E-Learning, 2*(4), 355-367. Retrieved on February 3, 2012 from http://www.wwwords.co.uk/pdf/validate.asp?j= elea&vol=2&issue=4&year=2005&article=5_Goodfellow_ELEA_2_4_ http://dx.doi.org/10.2304/elea.2005.2.4.355

Goodyear, P., Salmon, G., Spector, J., Steeples, C., & Tickner, S. (2001). Competences for online teaching: A special report. Educational Technology Research and Development, 49, 1, 65-72. http://dx.doi.org/10.1007/BF02504508

Hara, N., Bonk, C. J., & Angeli, C. (2000). Content analysis of online discussion in an applied educational psychology course. *Instructional Science, 28*, 115-152. http://dx.doi.org/10.1023/A:1003764722829

Haughey, D. J. (2007). Ethical relationships between instructor, learner and institution. *Open Learning, 22*(2), 139-147. http://dx.doi.org/10.1080/02680510701306681

Hollenbeck, C. R., Zinkhan, G., & French, W. (2005). Distance learning trends and benchmarks: Lessons from an online MBA program. *Marketing Education Review, 15*(2), 39-52.

Howell, S., Saba, F., Lindsay, N., & Williams, P. (2004). Seven strategies for enabling faculty success in distance education. *The Internet and Higher Education, 7*(1), 33-49. http://dx.doi.org/10.1016/j.iheduc.2003.11.005

Kreber, C., & Kanuka, H. (2006). The scholarship of teaching and learning and the online classroom. *Canadian Journal of University Continuing Education, 32*(3), 109-131. Retrieved January 27, 2012, from http://www.ccde.usask.ca/cjuce/articles/v32pdf/ 3225.pdf

Krieger, K. M., & Stockton, R. (2004). Technology and group leadership training: Teaching group counseling in an online environment. *The Journal for Specialists in Group Work, 29*, 343-359. http://dx.doi.org/10.1080/01933920490516044

Laat, M., Lally, V., Lipponen, L., & Simons, R. (2007). Online teaching in networked learning communities: A multi-method approach to studying the role of the teacher. Instructional Science, 35, 3, 257-286. http://dx.doi.org/10.1007/s11251-006-9007-0

McCracken, H. (2002). The importance of learning communities in motivating and retaining online learners. In V. Phillips, B. Elwert, L. Hitch, & C. Yager (Eds.), Motivating and retaining adult learners online (pp. 65-74). Retrieved January 25, 2012, from : www.geteducated.com

McShane, K. (2004). Integrating face-to-face and online teaching: Academics role concept and teaching choices. Teaching in Higher Education, 9(1), 3-16. http://dx.doi.org/10.1080/1356251032000155795

Olt, M. (2002). Ethics and distance education: Strategies for minimizing academic dishonesty in online assessment. *Online Journal of Distance Learning Administration, 5*(3), 1-7.

Palloff, R. & Pratt, K. (2005). *Collaborating Online: Learning Together in Community.* San Francisco, CA: Jossey-Bass.

Palloff, R., & Pratt, K. (2001). *Lessons From The Cyberspace Classroom: The Realities Of Online Teaching.* San Francisco, CA: Jossey-Bass.

Parlangeli, O., Marchigiani, E., & Bagnara, S. (1999). Multimedia systems in distance education: Effects of usability on learning. *Interacting with Computers, 12,* 37-49. http://dx.doi.org/10.1016/S0953-5438(98)00054-X

Rogers, C. R. (1951). *Client-centered therapy.* Boston, MA: Houghton Mifflin.

Sileo, J. M., & Sileo, T. W. (2008). Academic dishonesty and online classes: A rural education perspective. *Rural Special Education Quarterly, 27,* 55-60.

Simpson, O. (2005). E-learning, democracy and social exclusion. In A. A. Carr-Chellman (Ed.) *Global perspectives on e-learning: Rhetoric and reality.* Thousand Oaks, CA: Sage.

Starratt, R. J. (2004). *Ethical leadership.* San Francisco, CA: Jossey-Bass.

Chapter 2

Fostering Group Cohesion and Building Community

in a Virtual Classroom

Kylie P. Dotson-Blake and J. Scott Glass

Counseling is a profession built on relationships between people. Group counseling in particular relies on the interaction between group members to enhance the impact of the therapeutic work. This group cohesiveness is viewed as a main factor in the development of a sense of community (Joyce, Piper & Ogrodniczuk, 2007; Breunig et al., 2008), and has been defined as the "bond that links group members to the group, the degree to which the members are attracted to one another and the group, and the unity a group has towards its members" (Wilson, 2005, p. 238). Cohesiveness is one of the key factors in the development of a group (Burlingame, McClendon & Alonso, 2011; Joyce, Piper & Ogrodniczuk, 2007), and an important variable for a variety of groups and different types of group processes (Smith-Ray, Mama, Reese-Smith, Estabrooks & Lee, 2011) Group cohesion is also a potent variable in counselor education with the power of cohesion and group relationships allowing counselor educators to develop challenging and supportive learning communities that promote student engagement with content, theory and practice.

Group cohesion is often characterized by group members as experiencing caring and comfort, a sense of belonging, and the belief that they are valued and accepted (Corey, 2004; Yalom, 1995). Within the group counseling field, it is widely asserted that greater therapeutic gains occur in groups displaying higher levels of group cohesion (Burlingame, McClendon & Alonso, 2011; Burlingame, Fuhriman, & Johnson, 2001). Ideally, as the group develops over time the level of group cohesion increases as bonds are strengthened and members engage in the process of developing trust with one another (Joyce, et al, 2007). As group members have the opportunity to share personal experiences with the group, cohesion is facilitated and members are able to identify more strongly with one another (Corey). Research has demonstrated that cohesive groups typically seem to outperform non-cohesive groups and have greater personal satisfaction (Evans & Dion, 1991).

Counselor educators, as well as group counselors, have long emphasized strong connections with students/clients in an effort to enhance the work being done in class and in group counseling (Shirk & Karver, 2011; Burlingame, et. al., 2011). In light of the professional scholarship stating that connections do matter within a therapeutic relationship (Shirk & Karver; Burlingame, et al., 2011), many questions arise. How does the incorporation of technology impact the counseling relationship and the training of future counselors? Does technology negatively impact the relationship-building processes between counselor and client? How might Counselor Educators utilize technology in a way that models for students the process of relationship-building in an era of technology?

There is little argument that within the past twenty years, the availability and popularity of communication tools, modalities, and social networking groups via the Internet have forever changed interpersonal communication (Lapadat, 2007). The human-centered, relationship-focused profession of counseling, though, has included counselors who did not consider themselves particularly tech-savvy. Though the number is likely growing as technology increasingly is integrated into our daily lives in the form of smartphones and tech-ready cars, in the past, few counselors would likely have identified as technophiles. Thus, the integration of technology into our training programs and counseling profession presents somewhat of a new, unexplored world for counselor educators. However, as social networking, Internet engagement and online education have become more popular, the manner in which institutes of higher education deliver distance education has been revolutionized and counselor educators are having to adjust to new processes, tools and expectations.

Though content and the foundational tenets and philosophies of counseling and counselor education are stable, the ways that this information is delivered to students and the ways in which students engage in learning opportunities within counselor education courses are evolving to include online delivery modalities and tools. What is clear then, is that though how information is delivered might change, there are some facets of counselor education that are critical and must be included if students are going to emerge from training as competent, prepared professional counselors. Relationship-building and cohesion are at the core of these necessary components. They are also a couple of the more difficult aspects for counselor educators with limited training in technology tools and strategies to maintain when modifying a traditional face-to-face course into an online delivery format.

One difficulty in having instructors make the switch from traditional face-to-face classrooms to virtual settings is that there are essential and perhaps new tasks that are needed for the material to be delivered effectively (Smith, 2010). For counselor educators who may emphasize group cohesion and a sense of connectedness in a typical classroom, the question remains, how can the same connectedness and cohesion among members be facilitated in a virtual setting where common methods of interacting and face-to-face discussions are not part of the learning landscape? In a face-to-face counselor education classroom, this process is facilitated, in part, by the power of group cohesion. This text seeks to share activities that allow counselor educators to promote the development of group cohesion and strong relationships within online professional development opportunities. In order to help instructors best understand how to utilize these activities within counselor education courses, it is necessary to first understand how to create an effective working environment, a connected learning community. Thus, this chapter will discuss, in depth, strategies to enhance group cohesion and build strong learning communities within online counselor education courses.

Fostering Group Cohesion in Online Learning Opportunities

As has been mentioned, the historical view of professors standing in front of classrooms and sharing information to be absorbed by eager students is changing. Lecterns are being replaced by personal computers, and traditional lectures are being swapped for podcasts and virtual learning worlds. In today's virtual classrooms, students and instructors are virtually present with one another in an online environment, but may no longer be physically present in the same environment (Jones, 2011). The worry among some educators is that the lack of face-to-face, personal contact with instructors and the other students will result in isolation that negatively impacts learning. Another key concern among educators is that students will not be encouraged to interact actively with each other in ways that allow the students to get to know each other and to develop trust in each other. Everyone has heard stories of online classes that simply provide information/content, ask students to read and review that information and then take a quiz or test to assess student learning. As counselor educators we recognize that one cannot simply "know enough" to be a good counselor. Developing into an effective counselor is a process that takes time, practice, engagement with other counselors and a great deal of personal reflection.

The key for counselor educators is to foster learning communities that support critical thinking while encouraging the development of group cohesion by emphasizing interaction with the instructor and other class members, supporting individual and collective learning, and promoting a sense of community and mutual support (Moisey, Neu, & Cleveland-Innes, 2008). These three critical tasks will be discussed in more detail below. However, it is important to recognize that, just like meaningful face-to-face classrooms, meaningful online learning communities are not the result of chance or by accident. It takes a great deal of intentional and thoughtful designing, planning, creating, facilitating and implementing on the part of the instructor for these types of learning environments to exist. For this to occur, it is critical that students feel as though they are a part of a purposeful community of learning (Liu, Magjuka, Bonk & Lee, 2007; Moisey, Neu, & Cleveland-Innes, 2008).

Emphasizing Interaction with Instructor and Classmates

Meaningful interactions between students and between students and instructor are necessary for building cohesiveness. In transitioning to online delivery of traditional course content, one mistake faculty make is to rely solely on course requirements that include many different assignments that are developed individually by students and submitted only to the faculty for review. Yes, these assignments allow the instructor the opportunity to gauge students' understanding of the content being presented in the course, much like questions asked by an instructor to the students in a face-to-face class, but they may do so at the expense of developing and fostering cohesion among students. A different way to gauge student learning while also emphasizing interaction with instructor and classmates is to utilize a discussion format around particular content-based topics. By requiring students to post responses not only to the instructor's initial prompt/question, but also to the responses of their colleagues, the instructor is able to both gauge student understanding of the material and also encourage the students to develop awareness of each other and each other's positions through increased interaction among students.

Supporting Individual and Collective Learning

Students' development of professional competencies in an online course can be promoted through a balance of individual and collective learning. Individual learning in online courses may be supported through reading of course materials, reflecting upon content, preparing literature reviews and other more typical individual student assignments. Additionally, individual learning in online courses may occur as part of the group process. When students are asked to reflect upon their engagement in group assignments and how they are making meaning of that group engagement, these reflections can lead to powerful individual learning.

Collective learning connections among participants, even participants in widely divergent parts of the state, country or world, in an online class are also certainly possible with intentional planning and thoughtful facilitation on the part of the educator. For example, McDonald and Gibson (1998) stated that learners in graduate courses were able to form cohesive, functioning groups using certain technology (computer-mediated conferencing). They found that rather than online interactions negatively impacting group development, instead group development continued to move through predictable phases into increased solidarity and involvement by group members. When conversations take place in an asynchronous format, students seem to appreciate the time they are given to reflect, and the lack of pressure to respond immediately. This time allows group members time and space to create appropriate responses that may enhance the level of support necessary to facilitate community building (Moisey, Neu, & Cleveland-Innes, 2008). There has even been some research suggesting that a greater sense of community in online learning may lead to improved academic performance (Overbaugh & Lin, 2006).

Promoting a Sense of Community and Mutual Support

In several ways, building online communities is similar to building communities anywhere, requiring leadership, social norms and relationships among participants (Kim, 2000; Palloff & Pratt, 1999). According to Palloff and Pratt (2005), there are five stages of collaboration for building online communities. The first stage requires that instructors or group leaders clarify the purpose and expectations for the online community. In the beginning of an online group, this involves working with group members to define the group's purpose and rules in an online class it includes explaining the purpose and expectations for the course. The second stage is defining the environment and explaining to group members or students where they will meet online (i.e., in a course discussion board, using a different online group conferencing tool, etc.). It is important in building an effective online community that instructors/group leaders clarify for students/group members, which areas and tools are available for private discussions and which are open to all students/group members. The third step is critical for the success of the online community and it requires skill on the part of the instructor/group leader. This step is to "model the process" (p. 22). It is necessary for the group leader/instructor to serve as a model for how to effectively collaborate online because many students may be unfamiliar with the process and unsure of how to gauge what works best. The instructor or group leader must continue to remain involved with the online community, guiding the process of engagement and collaboration and this is the fourth step. The final step, evaluation, is one that is necessary to maintain the ongoing success of the online community. By continually evaluating the group's processes and effectiveness, the instructor/leader is able to make changes necessary to align the group's efforts and expectations with the developmental levels of group members. Palloff and Pratt's stages of collaboration are helpful strategies to utilize to promote a sense of community and mutual support.

Building Online Group Cohesion: Getting to Know Oneself and One's Classmates

Brown (2001) found that students who felt connected to the class and other class members placed a high priority on the class and dedicated the appropriate time required to get to know others and learn from them. This suggests that those counselor educators who can create the greatest level of connection with and among class members may experience the greatest levels of interaction and sense of community. This is particularly true in online learning communities where it is easier for individuals to maintain a sense of anonymity and isolation from other class members without intentional, thoughtful planning on the part of the faculty.

Instructors would do well to know the class make-up in terms of new and returning students. It is likely in online courses, just as in face-to-face courses, that returning students begin the class with stronger connections to other returning students in the course and an enhanced sense of comfort and confidence. While returning students may be able to continue friendships in online courses that were started in previous courses, new students may find the process of meeting and interacting with others in a virtual environment to be daunting. Whereas new students may make small talk and introduce themselves in a face-to-face class, they may not be as comfortable or know how to effectively interact when they are in an online learning environment. Additionally, it is imperative that instructors seek to create opportunities for small talk and informal connecting which might not organically arise in online learning. Opportunities such as hosting an informal blog discussion about topics of professional interest or creating a forum that allows students to exchange resources they identify over the course of the semester or share social networking opportunities available to students allow students to connect with each other in order to facilitate the students' getting to know and trust each other. Building connections and trust is critical for group cohesion.

Brown (2001) did find that returning students could help or hinder the formation of an online community. When returning students interacted with new students the sense of community was enhanced, but when these students kept to themselves the formation of community was stalled. Therefore, it is important for instructors to understand the composition of the class and to clearly communicate expectations regarding engagement, discussion, partnering, etc. with students. It is also helpful for returning students in counselor education to understand they are to model expected behavior so that new students may follow their examples regarding interaction and investment in the class.

Once an instructor understands how much experience students have had with online learning and how familiar they are with each other, efforts to attend to the developmental needs of the online learning community can proceed. For example, three different courses requiring basic student introductions, no matter how technologically advanced those introductions are or what cool tech tools are integrated into the introduction assignment, with the same group of students does not add much in the way of enhancing group cohesion. If students have to introduce themselves time and again to the same people, it becomes monotonous and does not add particular meaning to the course. However, if student introductions are necessary because different faculty teaching each of the different courses, perhaps, the introduction assignments could be developed in a way that is specifically meaningful for each course in terms of content and focus. In the example of multiple introductions, faculty teaching the counseling theories course might choose to have students prepare brief videos introducing themselves and sharing what theorist they would be most likely to seek out as a client and why. This way the faculty member still gets to "meet" the students, but the other students don't automatically discount the assignment as redundant and instead will learn something unique about their classmates, which helps to build a sense of connectedness. The most critical point is that counselor educators must seek with each group activity that is used in online learning to consider how it helps the class connect as a learning community, how it helps the students learn content and how either of these areas may need to be strengthened.

Building Group Cohesion: Intentionality and Planning

For counselor educators who teach online courses, it is important that they be intentional about creating opportunities for students to interact, recognize commonalities, and share. These interactions can go a long way in developing connections and helping participants feel comfortable in the class. The key then is for instructors to effectively choose online activities that enhance learning while building relationships. The activities chosen and utilized in the course must be tied to the content and purposeful for the growth of the group. If the instructor is not able to identify an activity and clearly explain the goals and objectives for the class, then perhaps the activity is no more than a time-filler. For example, an effective assignment tied to course goals for an online family counseling course could be an assignment that requires students to follow the blog of a well-known family counselor and then discuss in the student's small online group how the blog focused on positive communication within the family. To further extend the learning opportunity, the instructor could require students to also practice some of the positive communication strategies discussed in the blog within their online group. An activity that would fall short and serve more as a time filler would be to have students simply search out blogs of well-known family counselors with no required reflection. Just as in counseling, it is important that counselor educators give thought as to why the activity is being used, how it applies to that particular group, and what outcomes are expected before the activity is implemented. Preplanning will help a lot in ensuring that activities meet the desired objectives. Most importantly, with thoughtful planning, counselor educators can integrate activities into their courses that are designed to promote ongoing engagement among students, allowing students opportunities to get to know each other and develop trust in each other. Furthermore, these activities can be designed to build upon the trust and relationships to develop a strong sense of community and group cohesion.

In counseling settings, trusting relationships are critical to the success of therapy. In counselor education courses, these connections can be utilized to form strong learning communities. For this reason, it can be helpful for counselor educators to have a number of activities they can use in online courses that can teach course content while helping to build community among participants. Brown (2001) emphasized the importance of shared purpose and trials and a climate of caring and effective communication for the success of online communities. Therefore, if instructors are cognizant of the fact that shared experiences help create communities, then the task becomes creating effective activities for the class members to participate in to enhance learning while building relationships. While it is common for counselor educators to infuse group activities into the curriculum in face-to-face classes, it is likely not as easy to transition those meaningful activities into a virtual learning environment. The activities presented in this this text are intended to be integrated into online counselor education classes and professional development experiences with the focus on building group cohesion, enhancing processing and in whole building and strengthening online learning communities. We hope that having a collection of experiential activities to use in counselor education online courses will enhance knowledge of the content while building group cohesion and a sense of community among participants.

References

Breunig, M., O'Connell, T., Todd, S., Young, A., Anderson, L., & Anderson, D. (2008). Psychological sense of community and group cohesion on wilderness trips. *Journal of Experiential Education, 30*, 258-261.

Brown, R. E. (2001). The process of community-building in distance learning classes. *Journal of Asynchronous Learning Networks*, 5(2), 18-35. http://spot.pcc.edu/~rsuarez/rbs/school/EPFA_511/articles/from%20 Erica/community%20building.pdf

Burlingame, G. M., McClendon, D. T., & Alonso, J. (2011). Group cohesion. In J. Norcross (Ed.). *Psychotherapy Relationships that Work (2nd Ed.)*. New York, NY: Oxford University Press. http://dx.doi.org/10.1093/acprof:oso/9780199737208.003.0005

Burlingame, G. M., Fuhriman, A., & Johnson, J. E. (2001). Cohesion in group psychotherapy. *Psychotherapy, 38*, 373-379. http://dx.doi.org/10.1037/0033-3204.38.4.373

Corey, G. (2004). *Theory and practice of group counseling (with InfoTrac)* (6th ed.). Belmont, CA: Wadsworth/Thomson Learning.

Evans, C. R. & Dion, K. L. (1991). Group cohesion and performance: A meta-analysis. *Small Group Research, 22*, 175-186. http://dx.doi.org/10.1177/1046496491222002

Jones, I. M. (2011). Can you see me now? Defining teaching presence in the online classroom through building a learning community. *Journal of Legal Studies Education, 28*, 67-116. http://dx.doi.org/10.1111/j.1744-1722.2010.01085.x

Joyce, A. S., Piper, W. E., & Ogrodniczuk, J. S. (2007). Therapeutic alliance and cohesion variables as predictors of outcome in short-term group psychotherapy. *International Journal of Group Psychotherapy, 57*(3), 269-296. http://dx.doi.org/10.1521/ijgp.2007.57.3.269

Kim, A. (2000). *Building community on the Web: Secret strategies for successful online communities.* Berkeley, CA: Peachpit Press.

Lapadat, J. C. (2007). Discourse devices used to establish community, increase coherence, and negotiate agreement in an online university course. *Journal of Distance Education, 21*(3), 59-92.

Liu, X., Magjuka, R. J., Bonk, C. J., & Lee, S. (2007). *Does sense of community matter? An examination of participants' perceptions of building learning communities in online courses.* The Quarterly Review of Distance Education, 8(1), 9-24.

McDonald, J., & Gibson, C. (1998). Interpersonal dynamics and group development in computer conferencing. *The American Journal of Distance Education, 12*(1), 7-25. http://dx.doi.org/10.1080/08923649809526980

Moisey, S. D., Neu, C., & Cleveland-Innes, M. (2008). Community building and computer-mediated conferencing. *Journal of Distance Education, 22*(2), 15-42.

Overbaugh, R., & Lin, S. (2006). Student characteristics, sense of community, and cognitive achievement in web-based and lab-based learning environments. *Journal of Research on Technology in Education, 39*(2), 205-223.

Palloff, R. & Pratt, K. (2005). *Collaborating Online: Learning Together in Community.* San Francisco, CA: Jossey-Bass.

Palloff, R., & Pratt, K. (1999). *Building learning communities in cyberspace:Effective strategies for the online classroom.* San Francisco, CA: Jossey Bass Inc.

Shirk, S. R. & Karver, . (2011). Alliance in child and adolescent therapy. In J. Norcross (Ed.). *Psychotherapy Relationships that Work (2nd Ed.).* New York, NY: Oxford University Press.

Smith, V. C. (2010). Essential tasks and skills for online community college faculty. New Directions for Community Colleges, 150, 43-55. http://dx.doi.org/10.1002/cc.404

Smith-Ray, R., Mama, S., Reese-Smith, J. Y., Estabrooks, P. A. & Lee, R. A. (2011). Improving participation rates for women of color in health research: The role of group cohesion. Prevention Science, 13, 27-35. http://dx.doi.org/10.1007/s11121-011-0241-6

Wilson, G. L. (2005). *Groups in context: Leadership & participation in small groups.* New York: McGraw Hill.

Yalom, I. D. (1995). *The theory and practice of group psychotherapy* (4th ed.). New York: Basic Books.

Chapter 3

Processing and Group Dynamics in an Online Environment

J. Scott Glass and Kylie P. Dotson-Blake

An important component of online courses is to present material in a manner that engages students while encouraging interaction and communication among group members (Daugherty & Turner, 2003). In addition, research suggests that patterns of group dynamics may impact student interaction and engagement. For example, one study demonstrated that group composition was an important factor impacting collaborative environments, (Oliver, Omari, & Herrington, 1998). In addition, the same study found that peer support and cooperation were critical in the learning process. Furthermore, learning outcomes may be influenced by comfort level with group members (Yaverbaum & Ocker, 1998). Understanding those aspects of group dynamics which may influence student outcomes can help counselor educators better design and implement online courses that will engage students, develop connections and enhance learning opportunities.

Trust is created when people listen and communicate effectively with one another, value one another, take time to invest in those relationships and foster an environment of caring for others. Focusing on communication by groups via the Internet, McConnell (2005) states that trust in the identity of those with whom you are communicating is critical to the development of a perceived community. The danger for counselor educators who teach online is the assumption that the technology alone will support the work of the group (McConnell) and as a result learning will occur along with a sense of community. Mantovani (1994) suggests that this is unlikely to be the case. Instead, successful use of the technology depends a great deal on the level of planning, preparation and implementation by the instructor (Fisher, Thompson, & Silverberg, 2005).

It has been stated that human beings function best in an environment that encourages free expression of emotion, and allowing persons to say exactly what is on their minds (Nathanson, 1992). It is important that instructors keep this is mind as they plan and develop their virtual classrooms. Just because the mode may vary, the needs of students remain similar. Therefore, it is important to recognize that the counselor educator has an influential role to play regarding the group dynamics displayed by the members of the online classroom.

Classrooms may form and develop in a similar fashion to how groups form. As participants are introduced to online environments, whether it be a returning online learner or a person taking an online course for the first time, it is likely that members do not know each other well and they each person is experiencing various levels of anxiety. Just as in the Forming stage of a group, leaders at this stage of the online course should choose low-risk activities, as safety is a priority (Thompson & White, 2010). In addition, at this time it is important for instructors should provide guidance to help facilitate a climate of support. Another suggestion would be for leaders to participate in activities at this time to model appropriate behaviors and help participants become more engaged (Thompson & White). These initial activities may include having students share information about themselves relevant to the content of the course. One example of an assignment appropriate for building group cohesion during the Forming stage is having students in a career development course make a video introduction of themselves in which they share the first career they remember wanting to pursue and how, if at all, they believe it relates to where they are at this point in their career trajectory. Having students discuss together their career dreams from childhood until the present day allows students to share about themselves as they are comfortable and helps them to start forming relationships with their classmates and group members.

In the second stage, Storming, instructors should stop activities to give participants time to discuss what is occurring. If members are arguing or fighting to find their places in the group, then the leader allows time for the group to discuss the relationships with each other. When leading a group, or a class, it is important for leaders to emphasize and enforce norms and expectations. Without this, the safety of the group can be compromised and the growth of the group may be in question. The Storming stage of group process for online learning communities can be facilitated by the strategies of establishing clear expectations and defining the environment put forth by Palloff and Pratt (2005). It has been demonstrated that modeling, encouragement, and participation by the instructor helped community form more quickly for students in online courses (Brown, 2001). Helping students effectively deal with issues, including those related to relationships and technology, should help them feel more connected and more comfortable with the online learning environment.

As the group moves into the Norming stage, the hope is that relationships will strengthen, trust increases and members become more willing to take risks. Here group leaders may feel more comfortable increasing the risk involved in the activities that are implemented. Self-disclosure may increase during the norming stage (Yalom, 1995), and instructors are likely to choose activities at this stage that push participants to share more with each other. The hope is that this will start to build connections among members and help participants find their role in the group (Thompson & White, 2010).

In the Performing stage, groups are functioning at a high level. Cohesiveness among group members has been achieved and trust is at its strongest point. It is during this time that group leaders may introduce higher-risk activities, which further push participants out of their comfort zones and encourages increased support for group members. Finally, it is important for counselor educators not to forget the significance of the Termination stage preferably referred to as the Closure stage. If an instructor has worked tirelessly to create a supportive, cohesive, caring environment, it would be a shame for the tasks involved as this stage in group development to be overlooked. Members should be given a time to prepare for the separation from the class, instructor and other group members. Each person should be given the opportunity to process what the end of the group means, and how she may be impacted by its closure.

In terms of the content that is discussed in classes, students develop more systematic comprehension when they are able to discuss what they read and it is connected to what they know from their own experiences (Fisher, Thompson, & Silverberg, 2005). This is the purpose of processing. Processing provides the opportunity for participants to take what they have learned, gain meaning from it in relation to themselves and the other group members, and apply it to their own unique situations. It is when the content becomes personal, and meaning is made from the experience. Some researchers have even described the processing component as the most important phase of group work (Jacobs, Harvill, & Masson, 1988). However, processing can be overlooked by some group leaders. Beginning group facilitators often emphasize the activities themselves rather than the processing (Glass & Benshoff, 1999). In online group activities the processing is critically important as it allows for students/group members to work together to make meaning of the activity and their participation.

Group processing has been defined as a review of a group session to describe actions by members that were both helpful and unhelpful in order to decide what actions to continue or change (Johnson, Johnson, Stanne, & Garibaldi, 2001). Processing activities and events that take place in group counseling helps group members better understand their experiences in the group and relate these to their personal lives. Glass and Benshoff (1999) stated that group activities and exercises must be followed by effective processing in order to have the greatest impact on the participants. Group leaders who involve participants in activities without taking time to process may be filling time without allowing group members to recognize the relationship between what they do in the group setting and their everyday lives. The same can be said of virtual learning settings. Instructors who engage students in activities without processing do not allow participants to maximize their learning. Regardless of whether the group is in a counseling setting or in a counselor education online classroom, successful facilitation involves more than simply engaging a group of people in a variety of exercises. It also includes helping group members examine what took place, and guiding them through a process of understanding and applying the lessons that may have been learned from the various activities.

Just as in face-to-face classes, counselor educators who teach online must spend time preplanning in order for class to run smoothly. Group activities that are used should be designed and chosen with specific goals in mind. For example, if a Counseling Skills class is learning about self-disclosure, then the activity used should encourage group members to share personal information, and allow opportunities for participants to discuss with each other what took place during the exercise. Intentionality is critical to ensuring that the activity relates to the course content being covered. The processing should be the link that connects the activity with the content of the course. Processing of activities becomes the bridge from exercise to insight (Glass & Benshoff, 1999). Without proper direction from the counselor educator, the learning intended to take place through the exercise may be lost on the participants, thereby minimizing the impact of the exercises.

PARS Model

One method of processing that can be adapted to work in an online environment is the PARS Model (Glass & Benshoff, 1999). The PARS Model (Processing, Activity, Relationships, Self) is comprised of three stages of processing, each with a possible focus on one of three specific areas. Processing includes three stages: Reflecting, Understanding, and Applying. The three specific focus areas are: Activity, Relationships, and Self.

FIGURE 1-The PARS Model

	Activity	Relationships	Self
Reflecting	*Reflecting-Activity*	*Reflecting-Relationships*	*Reflecting-Self*
Understanding	*Understanding-Activity*	*Understanding-Relationships*	*Understanding-Self*
Applying	*Applying-Activity*	*Applying-Relationships*	*Applying-Self*

Reflecting, the first stage, allows the participants the opportunity to retrace the steps of a particular exercise. Here the group answers the question, "What did we do?" During this stage the group members will share their perceptions of what took place, come to an agreement about what occurred, and begin to raise some issues that may have developed as a result of the experience. In this stage, members learn that although everyone participated in the same activity, each individual may have experienced the exercise differently and has a unique perspective on the actions of the group. During this stage, those perceptions are exposed, examined, and explored. Typically this stage is non-threatening to group members and fosters an environment where participants feel safe sharing and makes disclosure in subsequent stages, where more sensitive information may be revealed, more likely.

Understanding, the second stage in the PARS model, refers to the process of having participants reflect on what occurred with the group during the activity. In this stage, the group leader helps members gain insight into group processes that took place during the exercise. Miller (1995) stated that during this stage participants examine cause and effect relationships of what was learned during the first stage. Thus, in this second stage, the primary task for group members is to identify, investigate, and analyze group processes that took place during the exercise. Sarason and Potter (1983) concluded in their study that the more people are aware of what they are experiencing, the more aware they will be of their own role in determining their success. In the *Understanding* stage, the group leader moves the group towards a better understanding of how the group worked together as a whole. During this stage, the group should make progress in the areas of developing trust and respect. Feeling comfortable enough to share one's views with others is important in this process, and learning to appreciate the views of other participants is a step towards gaining respect for other group members.

The third stage of the PARS model is *Applying*. During this stage, group members are challenged and encouraged to apply what they have learned through the experience in the group to their relationships and activities outside the group. This stage is critical for the success of the group process because it is during this time that the relevance of the activity is examined. Each member may come from a different background, and in this stage each individual is helped to learn how to apply the information from the previous two stages in his or her daily life, away from the group. For example, if the group has worked on problem-solving techniques, members might learn how to peacefully resolve disagreements within the group, and therefore better understand how to solve such disputes in their everyday lives. *Applying* questions help group members recognize the impact and purpose of the activity, because it is what they take back to their personal lives that can make a difference.

In addition to the three stages, the process model includes three areas of focus for the processing experience (the ARS in the PARS model): Activity, Relationships, and Self. In each focus area, intentional questions (See Appendix A) are used to enhance group discussions while helping members learn more about themselves and others and how the various activities can benefit them. *Activity* focus directs attention to the activity or event experienced, emphasizing the perceived facts of what happened. *Relationships* focus asks participants to consider what occurred and to reflect on the interactions that took place related to the activity. Finally, *Self* focus involves having participants examine closely their own roles and behaviors that were part of the group experience and the effects of that experience on them personally.

While the PARS Model was created to be used as a guide to help group leaders effectively process with their groups, it is important to note that it was not intended to be followed consistently as a step-by-step, sequential process. It is beneficial for group leaders, and counselor educators to possess appropriate facilitation skills, so they may move through the model in the manner in which the group leads them. It is important to keep in mind that it is simply a model or guide for processing, and the most effective facilitators will take their cues from the group itself. For example, if the leader begins processing by discussing Reflecting-Activity questions, and the group begins to examine topics addressed in the Understanding-Self section, the group leader should follow the conversation.

For online counselor educators, it is important that a great deal of time be spent planning, preparing and implementing their courses. Great learning environments rarely happen by accident, and effective instructors are those who understand this and effectively plan to reach learning goals for their classes. A part of successful online instruction includes using innovative methods of disseminating information and engaging distance learners. It is not enough to simply have a group of students engage in an activity. Instead, counselor educators must be intentional about choosing activities that help make the content understandable and applicable. It seems reasonable that instructors would choose activities based on the material being discussed. Just as group counselors should have clear goals and reasons for using certain activities in counseling, so should counselor educators. If instructors cannot point to clear objectives, what then is the point of engaging in the activity to begin with?

In addition to being intentional about which activities to use, counselor educators must also be sure to devote appropriate time to the processing of activities that are implemented in class. Processing aids participants in understanding the purpose of activities, and provides them with the opportunity to make meaning of the activity, both on a group and individual level. Without effective processing, the group may have been entertained and time may have been filled, but learning on a more in-depth level is lost. Those instructors who want to get the most out of their courses and the activities they have their classes engage in spend time planning (for the class and activities to be used), presenting (giving clear directions so participants are aware of responsibilities and expectations), and processing (in-depth examining of activity to gain meaning).

References

Brown, R. E. (2001). The process of community-building in distance learning classes. *Journal of Asynchronous Learning Networks*, 5(2), 18-35. http://spot.pcc.edu/~rsuarez/rbs/school/EPFA_511/articles/from%20 Erica/community%20building.pdf

Daugherty, M., & Turner, J. (2003). Sociometry: An approach for assessing group dynamics in web-based courses. *Interactive Learning Environments, 11*(3), 263-275. http://dx.doi.org/10.1076/ilee.11.3.263.16547

Fisher, M., Thompson, G. S., & Silverberg, D. A. (2005). Effective group dynamics in e-learning: Case study. *Journal of Educational Technology Systems, 33*(3), 205-222. http://dx.doi.org/10.2190/YTJ7-PLQB-VNDV-71UU

Glass, J. S., & Benshoff, J. M. (1999). PARS: A processing model for beginning group leaders. *Journal for Specialists in Group Work, 24*(1), 15-26. http://dx.doi.org/10.1080/01933929908411416

Jacobs, E., Harvill, R., & Masson, R. (1988). *Group counseling: Strategies and skills.* Pacific Grove, CA: Brooks/Cole.

Johnson, D. W., Johnson, R. T., Stanne, M. B., & Garibaldi, A. (2001). Impact of group processing on achievement in cooperative groups. *The Journal of Social Psychology, 130*(4), 507-516. http://dx.doi.org/10.1080/00224545.1990.9924613

McConnell, D. (2005). Examining the dynamics of networked e-learning groups and communities. *Studies in Higher Education, 30*(1), 25-42. http://dx.doi.org/10.1080/0307507052000307777

Mantovani, G. (1994). Is computer-mediated communication intrinsically apt to enhance democracy in organizations? *Human Relations, 47*(1), 45-62. http://dx.doi.org/10.1177/001872679404700103

Miller, D. (1995). Group facilitating. *Camping Magazine, May/June,* 28-32.

Nathanson, D. (1992). *Shame and pride: Affect, sex, and the birth of the self.* New York, NY: W. W. Norton & Company.

Oliver, R., Omari, A., & Herrington, J. (1998). Exploring student interactions in collaborative World Wide Web computer-based learning environments. *Journal of Educational Media and Hypermedia, 7,* 263-287.

Palloff, R. & Pratt, K. (2005). *Collaborating Online: Learning Together in Community.* San Francisco, CA: Jossey-Bass.

Sarason, I., & Potter, E. (1983). *Self-monitoring, cognitive processes, and performance* (Rep.) Seattle: University of Washington.

Thompson, P., & White, S. (2010). Play and positive group dynamics. *Restorative Practices, 19*(3), 53-57.

Yaverbaum, G. J., & Ocker, R. J. (1998). *Problem solving in the virtual classroom: A study of student perceptions related to collaborative learning techniques.* ERIC ED427750.

APPENDIX A

PARS Processing Questions

Reflecting–Activity

1. What did we do during this activity?

2. What was the hardest part of this exercise?

3. What was the easiest part of this activity?

Reflecting–Relationships

1. How did we act towards each other during this experience?

2. What kinds of things did we say to each other while we were doing the activity?

3. How did we as a group work through the activity?

4. What did we do during this activity to help each other?

5. Who emerged as a leader during this exercise?

Reflecting–Self

1. How did you as an individual participate in this activity?

2. Were you a help or a hindrance to the success of our group during this exercise?

3. What role did you assume in the group during this activity?

4. What did you do during this activity that you are most proud of?

5. What did you do during this activity that you are most disappointed in?

Understanding–Activity

1. Thinking about how we performed on the last exercise, what does this say about our group?

2. What did we learn about our group on the previous activity that we did not know before?

3. After observing how we performed on the last activity, what do you believe are the strengths and weaknesses of our group?

4. What is the purpose of our participating in this activity?

5. How will this activity benefit our group members?

Understanding–Relationships

1. Considering what we said earlier about our group, what does this say about our ability to work with others in the group?

2. How well does our group work together?

3. How efficient are we as a group at solving problems?

4. How well does our group work together at accomplishing a common goal?

5. Is our group able to put aside differences in order to succeed?

6. How well is our group able to listen to one another and share ideas?

7. How will working together benefit our group?

Understanding–Self

1. Considering what you said earlier about your participation in the group activity, what have you learned about yourself that you perhaps did not know before?

2. Viewing how you performed during this exercise, what does this say about your investment in this group?

3. Do you feel that you acted in a manner that demonstrates how important the success of this is to you?

4. How does participation in these activities benefit you as an individual?

Applying–Activity

1. What have we learned from participating in this particular activity that will benefit us in our daily lives?

2. What skills did we use during this activity that we may use back in the "real world?"

Applying–Relationship

1. What did our group do well in dealing with each other, that could benefit the individual members of our group back in school/work/home?

2. What skills did we use with each other that will help us with other people back in our daily environments?

3. What have we learned about working with others that will help us in other situations?

Applying–Self

1. What have we learned about ourselves that may affect how we handle other situations in the future?

2. What will you do differently as individuals back in your daily routines that will be a result of what you have learned here?

ACTIVITIES for MULTICULTURAL COUNSELING

Chapter 4

Exploring Whiteness and Microaggressions

in the Counseling Relationship

Natoya Haskins and Anneliese A. Singh

Goals and Learning Objectives:
1. Learn about theories of Whiteness and microaggression
2. Understand how theories of Whiteness and microaggression influence the helping relationship
3. Engage in a counseling dyad role-play exploring Whiteness and microagression

The learning objectives of the activity are:
1. Students will be able to identify how Whiteness impacts cross-cultural dyads
2. Students will be able to identify microaggressions taking place within the counseling relationship
3. Students will be able to broach issues in the counseling relationship related to Whiteness and microaggressions

Appropriate Course(s): Helping Relationships, Social and Cultural Diversity, Assessment

Point in Group When Activity is Used: This activity should be used either in the middle or late part of the class so that students and faculty have had adequate time to build some level of familiarity and trust with one another.

Estimated Time Length: 45 – 60 minutes

Technology and/or Materials Needed: The instructor should distribute the White Privilege Checklist adapted from Peggy McIntosh's article (McIntosh, 1988) prior to class discussion and the YouTube video (listed below) – both of which explore White Privilege. The instructor will refer to these resources during the online class to support and facilitate class discussion on Whiteness and microaggressions in the counseling relationship. GoogleDocs will be used as a means to share information during the activity.

Directions for Activity:

1. The instructor will provide a brief outline of Whiteness Theory and its impact on the helping relationship:

> Whiteness allows for extensive privilege to Whites. The curriculum emphasizes ideas and thoughts that serve to primarily enhance White students' success (Kozol, 2005) and often fails to address issues such as microaggressions that students of color experience when working with white clients. Microaggressions include verbal, behavioral, and environmental exchanges, whether intentional or unintentional, which communicate hostile, derogatory, or racial slights and insults that can negatively impact educational experiences (Sue, et al., 2007).

2. The class will then view Microaggression Video http://www.youtube.com/watch?v=BJL2P0JsAS4 and the facilitator will present the following case study:

> Marta is a counseling intern working at a counseling agency. After several sessions Marta believes she is experiencing microaggressions. She goes to her supervisor for consultation. She explained that yesterday her white male client expressed frustrations about being pulled over by a police officer for speeding. H e was surprised at how nice a Black police officer could be. He stated, "He must have been one of the more middle class conservatives. You know, like you…" She was slightly offended but didn't feel comfortable addressing it because she did not want to seem too sensitive.

3. The facilitator will simultaneously post the following questions for students to answer after viewing the video and reading the case study:
- Identify what microaggressions were present in the video and case study
- Identify how White privilege and Whiteness may play a role in this counseling dynamic
- Identify how the counselor might have addressed these microaggressions
- Discuss how the counselor might address differences and privilege during the initial session
4. Students will share these responses via a "GoogleDoc", which the facilitator will set up and invite all students to join using their college/university emails prior to the class beginning
5. The facilitator will then ask the students to read the responses of their classmates

Discussion/Processing Questions:

1. How has Whiteness and White privilege effected your interactions with clients
2. Describe a time when you experienced microaggressions in the helping relationship
3. What is a cultural competent way to address differences and microaggressions with clients

Potential Adaptations: The following adaptations may be made for persons with disabilities:

1. In accessing the YouTube video, visually-impaired or low vision students, assistive technologies may be used in tandem with ACCESSYouTube (http://edu.mwjt.co.uk/access-youtube-new-website-to-simplify-youtub). This website also provides mouseless browsing capabilities.
2. For the GoogleDoc and White Privilege document (McIntosh, 1988), visually-impaired or low vision students may use assistive technologies that they use for general computing tasks
3. For students with hearing disabilities, closed captions will accompany the YouTube video (www.youtube.com/t/captions_about)

Cautions/Potential Issues: When implementing this activity, the following considerations should be taken into account:

1. Explain that students must turn up the volume and ensure that the volume icon is not on "mute" when accessing the YouTube
2. Ask that students have access to a Gmail account in order to access the documents uploaded on GoogleDocs

Credits/References:

Haskins, N. H. (2012). White faculty preparing students of color to counsel white clients. Manuscript Under Review.

Haskins, N. H. (2011). *A critical look at minority student preparation to counsel white clients* (Doctoral dissertation). Retrieved from Dissertations and Theses database. (UMI No. 3472226).

Kozol, J. (2005). *The shame of the nation: The restoration of apartheid schooling in America.* New York, NY: Three Rivers Press.

McIntosh, P. (1998). Unpacking the invisible knapsack. Retrieved from www.nymbp.org/reference/WhitePrivilege.pdf

Singh, A. A., & Salazar, C. F. (2010). The roots of social justice in group work. *Journal for Specialists in Group Work, 35*(2), 97-104.

Singh, A. A., & Salazar, C. F. (2010). Six considerations for social justice group work. *Journal for Specialists in Group Work, 35*(3), 308-319.

Sue, D. W., Capodilupo, C. M., Torino, G. C., Bucceri, J. M., Holder, A. M., Nadal, K. L., & Esquilin, M. (2007). Microaggressions in everyday life: Implications for clinical practice. *American Psychologist, 62*(4), 271–286.

Contributing Author(s): Dr. Natoya Haskins is an assistant professor at The University of Georgia in the Department of Counseling and Human Services. Over the last 8 years Dr. Haskins has worked as a school counseling director and school counselor in middle and high schools. In addition, she has spent time serving in the U.S. Army as a military police officer in Iraq and Kuwait. Her current research interests include the following: Whiteness Theory, Critical Race Theory, students of color counseling training experiences, school counselors 'advocacy interventions with special populations, and school counselor advocacy instrument development.

Dr. Anneliese A. Singh is an assistant professor in the Department of Counseling and Human Development Services at The University of Georgia. Her group experiences and interests include: social justice and group work, LGBTQQ youth and adults, Asian American/Pacific Islander group counseling, multicultural counseling and social justice training, qualitative methodology feminist groups with survivors of trauma. Dr. Singh is the Past-President of the Association for Lesbian, Gay, Bisexual, and Transgender Issues in Counseling and the current President-Elect of the Southern Association of Counselor Education and Supervision. She is the chair of the ASGW Human Rights and Social Justice committee. Dr. Singh is a co-author of *Qualitative Inquiry in Counseling and Education.*

Chapter 5

Your New Tattoo

James M. Benshoff

Goals and Learning Objectives:

1. Icebreaker activity
2. Help group members creatively introduce themselves and share something about themselves with the group
3. Increase group members' comfort with self-disclosure within the group

Appropriate Course(s): Introduction to Counseling, Social and Cultural Counseling, and Group Counseling

Point in Group When Activity is Used: This activity is appropriate for use at various points in a class or group, depending on level of depth desired by instructor. It can be an effective introductory exercise at the beginning of a class to get students to self-disclose and get to know one another, but it is likely that level of disclosure will be less in-depth. It can also be implemented later in a course as a means of facilitating group cohesion and encouraging greater levels of disclosure.

Estimated Time Length: 20-30 minutes depending on size of group and selected approach to generating and sharing tattoo.

Technology and/or Materials Needed: Materials needed can vary depending on how simple or complex the instructor wants to make the activity. For example, group members could simply be asked to describe their tattoo using a group blog in a text-only format. In this case, no special materials or accommodations, beyond access to a computer, are needed. Alternative approaches to this could include: (1) asking group members to draw or assemble their tattoo (e.g., between class meetings), take a photo of it, and post the photo online during the group meeting for others to view, or (2) using a webcam, group members could sketch their tattoo in a synchronous group meeting and then share it using the webcam. Ideally, class members would have paper and crayons or colored markers at hand to prepare the image of their tattoo. In an asynchronous format, clients could post a photo of their tattoo along with written responses to questions listed in the directions below to share with others. These could easily be posted on a website or learning platforms like Blackboard, or a group blog (Blogspot.com).

Blogspot.com is a provider of free blog pages. Any individual or group leader can create a page by simply creating a free account.

Directions for Activity: Specific posted directions may include the following:

Imagine that one requirement for being in this group is that you have to get a tattoo in recognition of being a part of this group. This is a requirement, so you can't choose <u>not</u> to get one. If you already have tattoos, you have to get a <u>new</u> one. Your tattoo can be any design, any size, and in any location on your body that you choose. Take a few minutes to create your tattoo (in your mind or on paper), and then I'll ask you each of you to share your tattoo with the rest of the group.

Provide time for group members to work on tattoo.

Please share your tattoo (verbally or visually) with the rest of the class/group. Talk about the following aspects of your tattoo:

- *Tell us about what the tattoo represents/means to you. What would you want it to "say" about you?*

- *What would be the size of the tattoo?*

- *Where would you place it on your body?*

- *Would you use colors or just one color of ink?*

Discussion/Processing Questions:

1. How did you feel about this activity?

2. What did you learn about other class/group members through this activity?

3. What did you learn about yourself?

4. How might you apply what you've learned about others or yourself to our work together in this group?

Potential Adaptations: 1. Group members could share tattoos with each other (in small group "rooms" online or through IM) and then report on their impressions/experience of the activity in large group. 2. Another adaptation would be using visual images to augment verbal descriptions of participants' tattoos. Images of individual tattoos could be posted online and design/concept could be revisited as part of termination of class to determine what might have changed in the time since participating in the activity at the beginning of the course. 3. Students work in small groups (online "breakout" rooms) to design a tattoo that represents their group. Small groups would then each share their tattoo and its meaning with the rest of the class. 4. Students could be asked to find tattoo images (or images that could be used to design a tattoo) online and then post one that is meaningful for each of them. Each student would take a turn displaying the found tattoo image online in class and discussing its meaning for him/her.

Cautions/Potential Issues: Some group members may not have access to webcams or digital cameras and/or are not familiar with using that kind of technology. If the leader decides to have participants draw/create tattoo to share visually, a fallback can always be to just use words to describe it (e.g., if most participants can use visual imagery but a couple cannot). As always, technological challenges are greater when doing this activity in a synchronous (real-time) online group meeting, because of internet connection and management issues. The easiest way to do this is simply to ask class members to describe their tattoo, but images can significantly enhance the experience for everyone. It is also suggested that the instructor(s) participate in this activity and share his/her own ideas; if needed, this could model appropriate level of disclosure for participants.

Credits/References: The author created this activity several years ago to use in face-to-face classes, and has since adapted it for use in his online teaching.

Contributing Author(s): Dr. James M. Benshoff is a professor in the Department of Counseling and Educational Development at the University of North Carolina at Greensboro. He is a convert to experiential learning, and enjoys the challenge of introducing creative ideas and teaching methods in his graduate courses. One of his primary areas of interest is group process and leadership.

Chapter 6

Understanding Self and Others

Lorraine J. Guth

Goals and Learning Objectives:

1. Participants will increase their awareness of their own unique characteristics such as cultural heritage, gender, socioeconomic status, abilities, sexuality, and spirituality.
2. Participants will increase their understanding and acceptance of others' diverse qualities.
3. Participants will improve effectiveness of communication with diverse cultures.

Appropriate Course(s): Social and Cultural Counseling

Point in Group When Activity is Used: This activity should be used at the beginning of the class when participants are getting to know each other.

Estimated Time Length: It will take 60-90 minutes for each participant in the online environment. Total time for the activity to be completed for the entire group will depend on deadlines set by facilitator and the size of the group.

Technology and/or Materials Needed: The activity is best facilitated in a Course Management System (CMS), Learning Management System (LMS), or Virtual Learning Environment (VLE) that has a discussion board or forum capability. This would allow participants and the facilitator to post comments and share ideas. Some examples of these systems would be Moodle (moodle.org), Desire2Learn (desire2learn.com), and Blackboard (blackboard.com).

Directions for Activity: This interactive, online activity is designed to have participants increase their awareness of themselves and others. This will be done by having participants share surface and deeper qualities in response to a series of questions that are posted on the discussion board. Participants will also make connections with others in the group.

<u>Introduction to Activity:</u> Before the activity begins, the facilitator should discuss the norms for the online class environment that would help to promote participant sharing and acceptance of each other. These norms may include confidentiality, respect for ideas, personalizing knowledge, and value risk taking/expressing emotion (Blumenfeld, 1993).

On the discussion board the facilitator could state, *"You'll be participating in an activity designed to get to know yourself and others in the class better. There will be a series of questions posed on this discussion board for you to answer. As you answer the questions in the order given, you will also be asked to connect to others in the group."*

The facilitator should pose the following questions/directives for participants to answer in the order asked. Each question/directive could be a different thread on the discussion board.

These questions/directives include:

1. What are five surface characteristics that you possess that someone who meets you in person could easily see?
2. Read the posts of other participants, and reply to two other people with whom you connect regarding a surface characteristic.
3. What are five deeper characteristics that you possess that someone who meets you in person could not easily determine?
4. Read the posts of other participants, and reply to two other people with whom you connect regarding a deeper characteristic.
5. If you do not connect with any of the other participants on the characteristics stated, post this on the discussion board so others can add more characteristics to see if connections can be found.
6. What are three things you want others to know about your identity (e.g. race, ethnicity, gender, socioeconomic status, abilities, sexuality, and/or spirituality)?
7. Comment on the posts of two other participants.

When this activity is over, the facilitator can then pose the following processing questions on the discussion board.

Discussion/Processing Questions:

1. What commonalities or differences do you notice in the responses from all participants?
2. How do the characteristics shared in all of the postings contribute to the overall identity and uniqueness of the class?
3. How do the responses relate to multicultural and diversity issues in counseling?
4. What feelings emerged for you during the activity?
5. What thoughts did you have as you engaged in the activity?
6. What have you learned from the activity?

Potential Adaptations: Appropriately adapted computer equipment or assistive technology may be needed for some participants who have disabilities.

Cautions/Potential Issues: It is important to establish the norms listed at the beginning of this activity related to confidentiality, respect, and acceptance. Facilitators must be aware of potential stereotypes and biases that could surface during the discussion board activity. Care must be taken to appropriately process any issues that surface and to reinforce the norms that were set at the beginning of the online course.

Credits/References:

Blumenfeld, W. J. (1993). *Homophobia: How we all pay the price.* Boston: Beacon Press.

Contributing Author(s): Lorraine J. Guth, Ph.D., is a Professor in the Department of Counseling, Indiana University of Pennsylvania. She teaches multicultural and diversity issues, group counseling, and group practicum courses for graduate counseling students. She has led or co-led a variety of counseling, personal growth, and psychoeducational groups. She has conducted numerous presentations on group work and recently presented on group counseling at the National Board of Certified Counselors International Counseling Conference in Thimphu, Bhutan. She has also published several articles on group work and serves on the Association for Specialists in Group Work Leadership team as the Awards Committee co-chair.

Chapter 7

Building Trust via Dialogue: Valuing the Relevance of Names

Sheila M. Austin, Gilbert Dueñas,

Glenda P. Reynolds and M. Carolyn Thomas

Goals and Learning Objectives:

1. Use primary sources, conduct research of your family name
2. Use secondary sources such as the internet, explore the popularity of your name.
3. Students will gain increased appreciation for the role that their names have within the family and local community.

Appropriate Course(s): Social and Cultural Diversity

CACREP Standard: G.2.b. attitudes, beliefs, understandings, and acculturative experiences, including specific experiential learning activities designed to foster students' understanding of self and culturally diverse clients:

Point in Group When Activity is Used: This activity is most effective if introduced in the second week of the school term. The instructor will ascertain that students have access to the technology required for the activity and provide instruction on the use of technology as needed. The activity will be utilized throughout the term.

Estimated Time Length: This is a unifying activity that will merge classroom instruction with experiential activities to inform students about the significance of their name and its traditional usage in society.   The following is a suggested timeline to introduce and implement the steps in this activity:

- Introduction of project – 20 minutes
- Student preparation – 2 hours
    - Interviews, review of course textbook, and online research
    - Individual presentations – 2-3 hours depending on the number of presentations

Technology and/or Materials Needed: These activities require the use of the Internet for finding background information of their name. Further, students will construct a one-slide PowerPoint, which includes a personal picture of the member and information about their name. Instructions for creating electronic posters can be found at Education Blogster (http://edu.blogster.com). Equipment includes:
Photo or video camera
Audio
PowerPoint
Computer
Projector or smart board

Directions for Activity: Using both primary and secondary sources, students will independently research the history and significance of their names and portray the exploration of their names via a creatively designed PowerPoint slide. The steps are:

1. Use the following web link, http://www.socialsecurity.gov/OACT/babynames/ and consult resources to create a one-slide PowerPoint that includes a personal picture(s) of your life and information about your name. Some suggested resources include:

Christensen, L. (2000). *Reading, writing, and rising up: Teaching about social justice and the power of the written word.* A Rethinking Schools Publication. Milwaukee, WI: Rethinking Schools, Ltd.

Cisneros, S. (1984). *The house on mango street.* New York: Random House, Inc.

Edinger, M. (2000). *Seeking history: Teaching with primary sources in grades 4–6.* Portsmouth, NH: Heinemann.

Potter, L. A. (2003). Connecting with the past. *Social Education, 67*(7), 372-377.

2. Give a 5-7 minute classroom presentation using technology tools such as Smartboard, Internet, and PowerPoint. Students will discuss what they learned. Working together in groups, students will create a PowerPoint presentation to discuss names in different cultures, how names are selected, meanings attached to names, and changes in names due to historical trends. If necessary, the teacher should give examples for students to start thinking about their presentation. Students need to discover the significance of this activity for themselves. These groups may meet during class or outside of class time.

3. The classroom teacher may use a grading rubric to assess the extent to which the student used primary sources to discuss the history of their name, personal pictures of their life, and relevant web sites as references for secondary sources.

Blohm, J. M., & Lapinsky, T. (2006). *Kids like me: Voices of the immigrant experience.* Boston, MA: Intercultural Press.

Winston, L. (1997). *Keepsakes: Using family stories in elementary classrooms.* Portsmouth, NH: Heinemann.

Discussion/Processing Questions:

1. What did you learn about your family name that you did not know before?

2. How do you think other members now feel about your name?

3. Why should others come to appreciate the history of your name?

Potential Adaptations: Technology available for visually impaired include Screen Reader's software that reads the contents of a computer screen, converting the text to speech. Another adaptation for persons with disabilities is Zoom Text. ZoomText Magnifier is an advanced screen magnification program that enlarges and enhances everything on the computer screen, making the computer easier to see and use.

Cautions/Potential Issues:

1. Students must have general knowledge of Microsoft PowerPoint.
2. Students must have Internet accessibility.
3. Desire to gain knowledge of why your name was assigned to you.
4. The group leader should be prepared to process information that may be upsetting to someone who discovers unexpected, unwanted information about his or her name.

Credits/References:

Blohm, J. M., & Lapinsky, T. (2006). *Kids like me: Voices of the immigrant experience.* Boston, MA: Intercultural Press.

Christensen, L. (2000). *Reading, writing, and rising up: Teaching about social justice and the power of the written word.* Milwaukee, WI: A Rethinking Schools Publication.

Cisneros, S. (1984). *The house on mango street.* New York: Random House, Inc.

Edinger, M. (2000). Seeking history: Teaching with primary sources in grades 4-6. Portsmouth, NH: Heinemann.

Glogster Edu. (2012). *Glogster poster yourself.* Available from: http://edu.glogster.com/

Potter, L. A. (2003). Connecting with the past. *Social Education, 67*(7), 372-377.

Social Security Administration. (2011). *Baby names.* Available from: http://www.socialsecurity.gov/OACT/babynames/

Winston, L. (1997). *Keepsakes: Using family stories in elementary classrooms.* Portsmouth, NH: Heinemann.

Contributing Author(s): Sheila M. Austin, Ph.D., Associate Dean and Department Head of Counselor, Leadership and Special Education; Auburn University Montgomery. Dr. Austin has a combined 37 years' experience in public education, leadership, and diversity training.

Gilbert Dueñas, Ph. D, Assistant Professor, Department of Early Childhood, Elementary and Reading; Auburn University Montgomery. Prior to his current teaching position, Dr. Dueñas completed a 30-year Air Force career and worked seven years as a third grade teacher at an inner city public school.

Glenda P. Reynolds, Ed. D., L.P.C., Professor, Department of Counselor, Leadership and Special Education, Auburn University Montgomery: Dr. Reynolds is experienced in online counselor education classes, diversity training, and experiential learning.

M. Carolyn Thomas, Ph. D, Professor, Department of Counselor, Leadership and Special Education, Auburn University Montgomery; Dr. Thomas, an ASGW Fellow, has been a counselor educator for 37 years. Her publication topics include group work with victims of family abuse, diverse populations and older persons.

Chapter 8

Clarifying Group Member Roles

Angela McDonald

Goals and Learning Objectives:

1. Develop novice assessment skills of group dynamics
2. Identify personal characteristics of individual group members
3. Recognize and respect differences among group members
4. Use effective communication skills in receiving and delivering feedback
5. Interpret how individual behaviors contribute to overall group process

Appropriate Course(s): Group Counseling, Helping Relationships, Social and Cultural Diversity

Point in Group When Activity is Used: This activity is typically offered towards the end of a course in order to ensure that group members have had ample opportunity to observe patterns of behavior regarding group members' roles.

Estimated Time Length: Individual group members will need adequate time to reflect and construct labels for the other group members' roles, approximately 20 minutes. Additional time is needed to collect web artifacts that represent each group members' role, approximately 30 minutes or longer depending on the size of the group. Posting the web artifacts and typing explanations for each group member's web artifact will take at least 30 minutes, possibly more depending on the size of the group. Total time for this activity is approximately two hours.

Technology and/or Materials Needed: Online discussion board that permits posting of images, audio clips, and other external media. This can be done using a blog (Blogspot.com), Blackboard, or any program allowing the sharing of materials and the ability to carry on discussions with group members. The online forum should have restricted access so that it is accessible only to group members and not visible to the general public.

Directions for Activity: In this activity, group members individually select web artifacts that metaphorically represent each group member's role in the group, as perceived by each member. A web artifact can be an image file or audio clip. After individually selecting a web artifact for each group member, all group members post their member artifacts to a group discussion board with an accompanying brief description of why each artifact was selected for each group member. All group members are engaged in a process of giving and receiving feedback about their perceptions of each other's roles in the group.

Inform the group that all group members will be sharing their perceptions of each other's roles in the group by metaphorically representing the members' roles with web artifacts. Specific posted directions:

For this activity, I want you to think about each group member's contribution to the group and the role that he/she played in the group. Select an artifact using web resources that metaphorically represents each group member. Examples of appropriate artifacts may include audio clips of music that meaningfully represent a group member's role or image files that visually depict a group member's role. You might metaphorically represent a group member's role by selecting a piece of artwork, a food, or an animal. For example, if you find one of your group members to be very complex, you might find an image of an intricately woven fabric representing the complexity of that group member's behavior or you may find an image of an onion with many layers that are peeled away one by one. You are to write a brief 2-3 sentences explanation of why you selected each artifact for each group member. After you have selected a web artifact and written a brief explanation for each group member post your work to the group discussion board. Make sure that the web artifacts are working and edit where needed. For example, make sure that all image files are visible and that all audio files are playable. After all group members have posted their explanations and web artifacts, read through each other's responses and post questions and comments to others' postings. Be sure to keep up with questions and comments that are made to your original post.

It is important that you be constructive in your selection of web artifacts and in phrasing your explanations. Feedback from others is an essential component of self-learning from others in group work. It is important that you understand how to meaningfully give and receive feedback.

Discussion/Processing Questions:

1. Were others' perceptions of your role in the group, as represented by the web artifact, similar or different to how you thought you were perceived?
2. Were there commonalities among members' perceptions of each other?
3. How do you like to receive feedback? Is giving others feedback easy or difficult?
4. Do you feel a stronger connection, or sense of cohesion with your fellow group members after completing this activity?

5. What have you learned about yourself as a result of being a member of this group?

Potential Adaptations: The discussion board posts can be threaded by group members uploading all of their web artifacts in one post, or individual threads for each group member can be created to which each group member posts his or her web artifacts only for the group member in each member-specific thread. Web artifacts can be varied for ADA compliance.

Cautions/Potential Issues: Giving and receiving feedback about group members' roles can be difficult. Group members should be instructed as to how to give feedback to others before engaging in this activity. Group norms that have been established related to disclosure and authenticity will impact this activity. The instructor should closely monitor the discussion board conversations and assist in processing conflict and misunderstanding if necessary.

The activity should not be done too early in the group's lifecycle as members' posts may not reflect the depth that posts made at later stages of group development would reflect.

Contributing Author(s): Dr. Angela McDonald is an Assistant Professor in the Department of School Administration and Counseling at the University of North Carolina at Pembroke. She has experience working with counseling groups in agency and college counseling center settings.

64

Chapter 9

Our Photos, Our Voices

Pamela C. Wells and Cristen Wathen

Goals and Learning Objectives:

1. This activity addresses the following CACREP 2009 Standards:

II.G.2.b Foster attitudes, beliefs, understandings, and acculturative experiences, including specific experiential learning activities designed to foster students' understanding of self -and culturally diverse clients;

II.G.3.e Foster counselors' roles in developing cultural self-awareness, promoting cultural social justice, advocacy and conflict resolution, and other culturally supported behaviors that promote optimal wellness and growth of the human spirit, mind, or body

2. Enhance group cohesion in an online environment.
3. Utilize technology to promote awareness of self and others.
4. Gain knowledge, skills, and awareness in multicultural identity.

Appropriate Course(s): Aiming to increase the connection among online students, this activity can be utilized for multiple courses in a counseling program. Instructors may modify the activity to fit a particular course or subject matter within a course. The authors have provided specific prompts for a Social and Cultural Counseling course.

Point In Group When Activity is Used: This activity could be used throughout the term or as instructor deems necessary/needed, particularly when a sense of cohesion is desired or deemed beneficial.

Estimated Time Length: The activity could be used throughout the semester; dependent on student engagement and length of time instructor wishes to use on processing questions. Limited time is needed to take photo and upload to site.

Technology and/or Materials Needed: Camera or cellular phone with camera capabilities; access to Internet; tutorial regarding how to upload photos to photosharing site (i.e. Flikr).

The purpose of the technology used is for students to take photographs and be able to share their thoughts and feelings with their peers. If students do not have a camera or a cell phone camera, they may be able to borrow a camera from the university or perhaps from a local library. Students may also choose online images (check for copyright permission) to share with students that represent what they are feeling.

Directions for Activity:

1. Faculty member will identify an online photo-sharing website (Flickr) and/or a technological interface on campus (i.e. Blackboard, Moodle) for students to upload photos/descriptions to. The faculty member will create this site in advance through their Blackboard (or other interface) course or online through a photosharing website. Faculty members can view tutorials for their particular interface and/or visit the Flickr website for information on how to setup these modalities and for information on how to upload photographs. Students can access this information in the same way. A link is provided to the Flickr tutorial website: http://www.flickr.com/tour/#section=upload

2. Students will be asked to reflect on their participation and involvement in their online class. Students may be given prompts to encourage deeper levels of reflection. Examples of these types of prompts include:

   Think about your experiences so far in this course. Connecting in an online environment can present itself with its own set of unique challenges. How are you feeling about your level of participation and involvement? Do you feel satisfied or dissatisfied about your level of connection with your peers?

   If activity is used for a multicultural class or multicultural component of a class, the prompts may be modified to include:

   Think about your own stage of cultural development. Think about the stories you have heard about or read about from your peers. How is your experience similar? How is your experience different? How can you connect to your peers and their stories of culture?

3. Students will then be asked to take a digital photograph that embodies their thoughts and feelings regarding the prompts or questions. For a Social and Cultural Diversity class professors might ask students to take photographs representing concepts like

privilege, freedom, stereotypes, labels, diversity, etc. It is important for students to recognize the confidentiality of others they may be photographing, etc. Therefore we suggest the following guidelines:

    a. Only submit photographs of yourself and/or of inanimate objects/animals.

    b. Remember that others view photographs shared and that confidentiality cannot be guaranteed. Don't share something that you don't feel comfortable sharing!

    c. Please choose photographs that are appropriate for the classroom environment.

Example photograph:

"This picture depicts loneliness. While reflecting on my cultural identity, I recognized that I did not know much about my background. Others in the class seem to have a vast amount of knowledge and experiences in this area. I feel left out."

4. Students will upload their photograph to an online photosharing or area on Blackboard/additional technological interface site.

5. Students are then asked to view their peers' photographs on the website. Students are instructed to comment on the different

photographs. Faculty may choose to limit the number of comments a student is required to make, particularly if the class is large.
Example reflection questions:
What emotions came up for me as I looked at the photographs?
Did I connect with certain photographs more than others? Why?
What assumptions am I making as I reflect on others' photographs?
What surprised me about the photosharing process?

6. Faculty may choose to comment on the photos as well, or they may choose to monitor photos and comments.

Discussion/Processing Questions: Professor will implement at least 3 to facilitate learning- (these may be turned into a reflective journal entry or paper, or students may be asked to share with the class the answers depending on the professor's focus).

1. What do you want others to know about your experience?
2. What are you trying say by using this picture?
3. What emotions were evoked when you uploaded your photo and knew others would see the photos and your description of it? What emotions were evoked when you knew others would comment on your photo?
4. What thoughts and feelings did you experience while viewing others photos?
5. What impact, if any, does your photo have on our group's level of cohesion?
6. What similarities or differences did you see in your photos and those of other group members?

Potential Adaptations: Professors will work with students through the ADA office of the university to provide appropriate technology or alternatives for this activity. Professors are encouraged to modify the activity in a way that is most beneficial for all students in the course to build cohesion. Activity may be adapted to use other forms of media to share thoughts and reflections (i.e., songs could be uploaded; students could also share through blogging). Professor and students may work together to best adapt for the online scenario.

Cautions/Potential Issues: Confidentiality is a major issue to consider when utilizing this activity. Students may use a login or screen name when uploading photos to increase security. Only the class members and instructor should have access to the password for the photosharing site. Also, the instructor should be honest with students regarding the Internet security issues and provide alternate options for those choosing not to participate based on this reason.

Professors must consider the safety and vulnerability of the students and monitor posts and photo uploads for professionalism, appropriateness, and support. Discussion should take place regarding the thoughts and emotions that might come up during the activity and directions shared on how to process and share them appropriately and safely.

Professors should check in with students before and throughout the activity and preemptively provide resources for students if they feel overwhelmed and need outside support.

Credits/References:

Suler, J. (2009). The psychotherapeutics of online photosharing. International *Journal of Applied Psychoanalytic* Studies, 6(4), 339-344.

Suler, J. (2008). Image, word, action: Interpersonal dynamics in a photo-sharing community. *Cyberpsychology & Behavior, 11(5),* 556-559.

Contributing Author(s): Pamela C. Wells is a doctoral student at Idaho State University. Pamela is a Nationally Certified Counselor and has worked in both student affairs and mental health.

Cristen Wathen is a doctoral candidate at Idaho State University. She is a member of ASGW and has experience working with groups, co-teaching group courses, and loves experiential group work. She is a licensed counselor in Idaho and has worked with trauma and survivors of crime, single parents, and college students in her counseling experience.

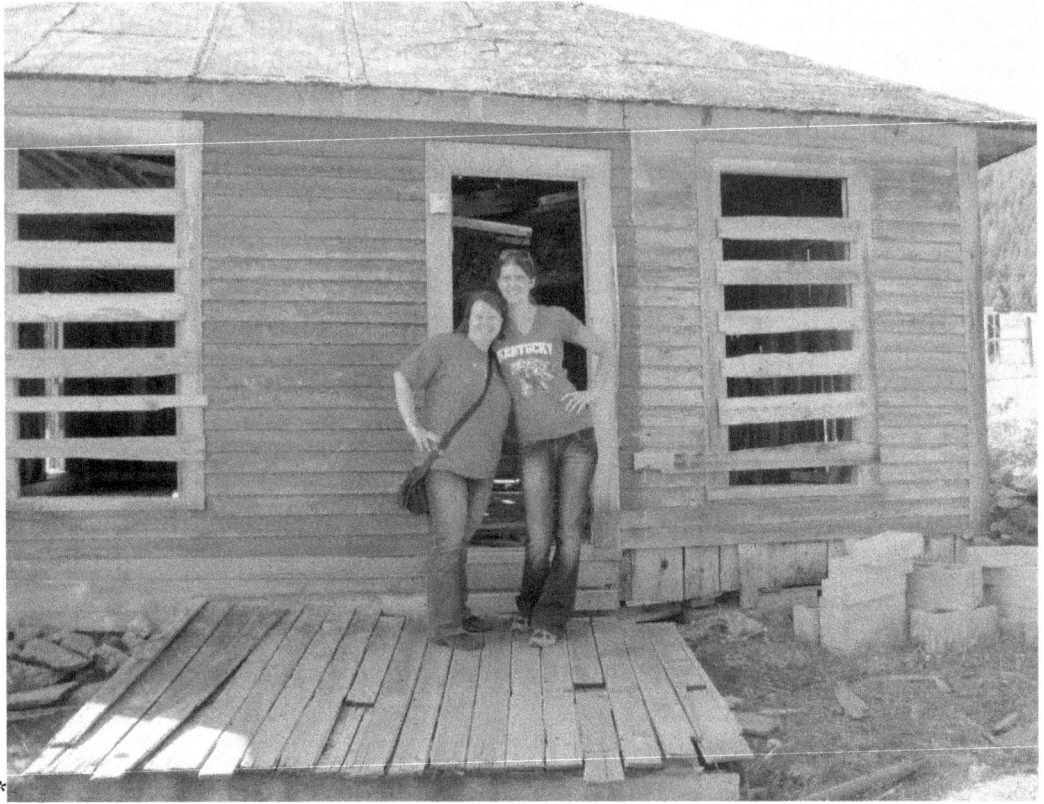

**

Chapter 10

A Different Island: Interacting with another Culture in

Second Life

Matthew T. Fish and Shari M. Sias

Goals and Learning Objectives:

1. Promote students' understanding of self and culturally diverse clients.
2. Provide students an opportunity to:
   a. become better acquainted with other cultures;
   b. explore personal beliefs and biases in the areas of communication styles and emotional expression when interacting with individuals perceived as different from themselves;
   c. address possible fears related to a lack of understanding or experience with a given culture.

Appropriate Course(s): Social and cultural counseling

Point in Group When Activity is Used: The activity is optimal in mid-semester. A level of trust is needed for students to identify and share their fears and biases, and engagement in this activity before that trust takes root will limit students' ability to share.

Estimated Time Length: Students spend at least 10 hours over the course of a semester interacting with a cultural group different than their own. Additional time may be needed to orient students to Second Life (SL).

Technology and/or Materials Needed: Students will need regular access to the Internet, high-speed DSL or cable modem Internet service, and a computer. Students will also need to download Second Life onto their computers.

Second Life is an online virtual world where users (also known as "residents") can interact and participate in individual and group activities. Creating residency on Second Life (an account) is free.

Directions for Activity: Before discussing the activity, basic terminology used in Second Life is explained and accessing SL is outlined. An avatar is a student's virtual representation in SL. This is a key component in keeping students involved. For instance, in a traditional distance education setting, students can leave their computers. However, when students are "inworld" on SL and their avatar is left unattended it will fall asleep (e.g., slump over) and others participating can see the avatar become disengaged. Avatars also vary from animals to virtual replications of the users (Boulous, Hetherington, & Wheeler, 2007). For the purposes of this activity, the authors suggest the latter.

A virtual world is the combination of avatars and islands. Islands are virtual land that can be purchased to erect buildings. Virtual worlds are digital environments accessed via the web where students, represented by avatars, communicate with each other and interact with the environment (Boulous, Hetherington, & Wheeler, 2007).

Simulation is a key aspect to the learning environment in SL. Kolb, Boyatzis, and Mainemelis (2001) found that simulations increase learning, retaining and recalling of concepts. Robbins and Butler (2009) found that performing real-life tasks in a safe virtual environment where feedback is given was a major benefit of this approach. Simulations can provide a degree of interaction and knowledge that other mediums in technology cannot. To illustrate, a Human Services Counseling Master's program used SL to teach counseling skills and students reported the simulated interaction was beneficial to their learning (Walker, 2009).

Accessing Second Life

Providing step-by-step guidelines for all SL processes is beyond the scope of this submission. However, tutorials for SL are provided on the SL webpage (www.secondlife.com) and at Second Life Wiki (http://wiki.secondlife.com/wiki/Video_Tutorials). The following information will get students started on SL. Students are encouraged to practice navigating this virtual world prior to visiting the "islands" of different cultural groups. Such practice may reduce problems in communication and interaction due to students' lack of comfort in a virtual world.

First, students will want to review and possibly print the Second Life Quick Start Guide, which can be accessed at www.secondlife.com. The guide provides an overview of 12 common tasks, such as how to change one's appearance; how to see and move in the SL environment; how to communicate (through local chats, voice chats, and instant messaging); and how to search for various locations. The guide also lists keyboard shortcuts which help expedite tasks.

Next, students will set up an account and install SL on their computers. They will develop a user name, a password, provide an email address, birth date, and a security question. Students will then choose from a selection of avatars, to which SL will direct them once they have set up their accounts. After an avatar is chosen, students are ready to explore SL.

Activity Guidelines

As noted earlier, there are three parts to this activity: researching a cultural group; interacting with the cultural group and keeping a reflection journal; and presenting what was learned to the class. Prior to their research, students need to understand the common elements of culture (i.e., social groups, social structure, customs, language, religion, daily activities, shared history, arts, government structure and economic structure). The following benchmarks should be used to guide students' writing: (a) Discuss why you've chosen a given culture. (b) What contact/experience have you had with this culture prior to SL? (c) Describe your chosen culture using the common elements of culture. (d) What new information did you learn from you research? The length of the research paper should be 7 to 10 pages.

Once their preliminary research is complete, students spend 10 hours over the course of the semester (typically two hours weekly) interacting with their chosen culture via SL. Interaction in SL increases the number of cultural groups from which the students can choose, and students should be encouraged to interact rather than observe. Examples of cultural groups –"islands" as they are known in SL - include persons from the deaf community (https://my.secondlife.com/groups/10af219f-73dc-f8da-b0be-4437d2f37144); persons from the LGBT community (http://secondlife.com/destination/persecution-to-pride); persons with differing spiritual beliefs and practices (for example, the Buddha Center [http://secondlife.com/destination/1066] or Spirit Nation [http://world.secondlife.com/group/faeba1ae-51f5-ff20-fe82-7734c0a0c364?lang=en-US]) as well as persons that are racially or ethnically different than the student. Examples of cultural immersion experiences are church-religious ceremonies, healing circles or pipe ceremonies, and interviews with persons not of one's own culture. To locate a culture or immersion experience, students need to consult the SL Destination Guide at http://secondlife.com/destinations?lang=en-US and the Destination Guide Frequently Asked Questions resource, which is located at http://community.secondlife.com/t5/English-Knowledge-Base/About-the-Second-Life-Destination-Guide/ta-p/700059.

Journals are written each time students interact with their chosen cultural group. The entries should not recount what students did but be descriptive in nature. Students are encouraged to relate their experiences to course readings and lectures and to explore times of discomfort or differences in values and beliefs. Students are to review their journals prior to class presentations to identify themes and areas of growth.

Students are encouraged to be creative when presenting what they've learned to the class. They may choose to "dress" their avatar in a way that represents their culture of study. Students may also choose to have classmates' participant in an activity such as a game from a given culture.

Discussion/Processing Questions: Discussion questions focus on the common elements of culture and on the students' beliefs, biases, and experiences. The following questions can facilitate class discussion after the student presentations:

1. What are some of the values and beliefs of the cultural group? How are these similar to your values and beliefs? How are these different from your values and beliefs?

2. What are some of the customs, explicit and implicit, of the cultural group?
3. How are issues of power managed in the cultural group?
4. What was the best part about the cultural immersion experience? Why?
5. What was the most difficult part about the cultural immersion experience?

Potential Adaptations: Adaptations to SL make it accessible to individuals with visual impairments. Adaptations include the use of haptic technology and TextSL. Computer haptics are software programs which use touch and vibrations to navigate virtual worlds (Castet & Florens, 2008). TextSL allows individuals who are visually impaired to use screen readers or talking web browsers to interact on Second Life (Folmer, Yuan, Carr, & Sapre, 2009).

Cautions/Potential Issues: Having students interact with another cultural group can be anxiety provoking. Some students find interacting on SL to be less anxiety producing than real-life interactions, but others report their discomfort and lack of experience with virtual worlds interfere with them being "truly present." That is, students were more worried/focused on technological concerns rather than the experience of being with a different cultural group. Students who fully explore and learn to adeptly navigate SL prior to the cultural immersion experience tend to report lower levels of technological anxiety.

Students who are new to virtual worlds are likely to require technical supports. Having course time set aside for training and using existing university supports such as information and technology (IT) support staff is encouraged.

Credits/References:

Boulos, M. N. K., Hetherington, L., & Wheeler, S. (2007). Second life: An overview of the potential of 3-D virtual worlds in medical and health education. *Health Information & Libraries Journal, 24(4)*, 233-245.

Castet, J., & Florens, J. L. (2008). A visual reality simulator based on hapics hard constraints. In M. Ferre (Ed.), *EuroHaptics* (pp. 918-923). Berlin: Springer-Verlag.

Folmer, E., Yuan, B., Carr, D., & Sapre, M. (Eds.). (2009). A command-based visual world interface for the visually impaired. Proceedings from the 11th International ACM SIGACCESS Conference on Computers and Accessibility. Pittsburg, PA.

Kolb, D. A. (1984). *Experiential learning: Experience as the source of learning and development.* Englewood Cliffs, NJ: Prentice-Hall.

Robbins, R. W., & Butler, B. S. (2009). Selecting a virtual world for learning. *Journal of Information Systems Education, Special Issue: Impacts of Web 2.0 and Virtual World Technologies on IS Education, 20(2)*, 199-210.

Walker, V. L.(2009). Using second life in counselor skill development. *Journal of Virtual World Research 2(1)*, 3-14.

Contributing Author(s): Matthew T. Fish, is a second year doctoral student in the Rehabilitation Counseling and Administration Program at East Carolina University in Greenville, North Carolina. Areas of specialty and interest include individual and group counseling with the active military.

Shari M. Sias, Ph.D., LPC, is an associate professor and Director of the Substance Abuse and Clinical Counseling Program in the Department of Addictions and Rehabilitation Studies at East Carolina University in Greenville, North Carolina. Areas of specialty and interest include group counseling with substance abusing clients, family counseling, and counselor development.

Chapter 11

Challenging Individual Assumptions through Avatar

Alison Sappie and Beth Vincent

Goals and Learning Objectives:

Identify the presence of individual stereotypes within all group members

1. Increase awareness of stereotypical thoughts and assumptions
2. Develop group cohesion by creating a connection through a shared experience
3. Provide introduction to ongoing process of developing and maintaining cultural competence in the counseling setting

Appropriate Course(s): Social and Cultural Counseling, and Group Counseling

Point in Group When Activity is Used: This group exercise can be implemented after a group has developed trust, cohesion, and mutual respect. This exercise would be most effective after students have developed familiarity with social and cultural counseling and been introduced to cultural competence.

Estimated Time Length: Before this activity is used, each individual member will need time to identify an unfamiliar cultural group and conduct research regarding members of the identified group. Once partners have traded descriptions, individuals will need 15-20 minutes (or longer based on familiarity with programs) to create an avatar based on the given description (could be done between class meetings). In addition, pairs will need 10-15 minutes to process their produced avatars and the group will need to process together as well.

Technology and/or Materials Needed: Group leaders will use an online discussion board or chat room to process and complete this activity (i.e., Blackboard). In addition group leaders will instruct members to create a virtual avatar through Voki (www.voki.com/create.php). Voki is a free online program used to create a 3 dimensional cartoon image of a person. Other online programs can be substituted to illustrate the human image.

Directions for Activity: Initial instructions for group activity preparation should include the following information:

We will be completing a group activity, which will also require you to work with a partner, which will be assigned. Your first task is to identify a cultural group that you have little to no previous knowledge about. Once you have identified a cultural group you will need to conduct research to educate yourself about the characteristics of the group. This research should go beyond basic facts and show deep insight into dimensions such as world view, values, customs, and familial dynamics. Gather information as if you were preparing to counsel a client from this background. Using the information from your research you will need to prepare a brief description of an individual who would identify with this culture. This description should not include <u>any</u> physical characteristics or information regarding gender. In addition, do <u>not</u> include which cultural group you are describing anywhere in on the post. Please write at least two well-developed paragraphs and post the description to the discussion board.

Once this preliminary task is completed instruction students to complete the following:

Please read your partner's post and using his/her description to create a visual representation of how you predict an individual matching this description would appear. Go to the Voki website (http://www.voki.com) and create an account before creating your avatar. Take your time and utilize as many of the customization tools available. Be as creative as possible. You can change the physical characteristics, the dress, and the background of your avatar. Explore the tabs beneath the avatar image to change the color and size of various physical characteristics. Once you have designed your avatar you will be directed by the website to give your avatar a voice. Use the "text to speech" button and type any phrase. Once this is complete click the publish button and title your avatar with your name and click save. To share your link with your classmates select the dropdown menu titled "Get Your Voki Link Here:" and click "standard Voki link". Copy and paste the URL in the discussion board as a reply to your partner's description.

After the group members have completed the instructed tasks begin processing the activity and use the following instructions:

Respond to your partner's avatar post on the discussion board. Please include your reaction to their creation. Were you surprised by your partner's interpretation of your description? Do you believe your description provided a clear representation of an individual from the cultural group you researched? Include any other reactions and be sure to include the cultural group you chose to describe. Please view at least two other discussion threads before participating in the group conclusion thread.

Discussion/Processing Questions:

1. Were you surprised by any similarities or differences between your interpretation and your partner's interpretation of the selected cultural group?
2. Did this activity make you aware of any biases or areas for improvement regarding your cultural competence as a counselor?
3. Did you notice any trends in interpretations when viewing the other group members' experiences with this activity?
4. How can you apply this experience to your future practice with diverse clients?
5. How do you feel your classmates represented your cultural group in this activity? In your opinion were the descriptions and avatars accurate representations of your cultural identity. If your cultural group was not represented do you feel you received accurate information from this activity?

Potential Adaptations: Group leaders can substitute other creative components to create the avatar. The tools for this exercise can be chosen based upon the platform of the group.

The group leader can instruct members to draw their avatar by hand and upload the image to the discussion board. This would require scanner, digital camera, or other means of uploading an image to the computer.

Cautions/Potential Issues: When using activities to identify biases and cultural naiveté there is often a risk for offending or isolating a group member. Group leaders need to be conscious and sensitive to this and outline clear rules for the group. In addition, technology can be challenging for some group members especially when using a new website such as Voki. It would be useful to encourage group members to leave ample time to complete this assignment to leave flexibility to work through any technological difficulty. Some students may be more apt to creating vivid descriptions while others may provide vague descriptions. Group leaders may wish to expand on the guidelines to ensure adequate detail is used when completing the assignment.

Contributing Author(s): Alison Sappie and Beth Vincent are both students in the Department of Higher, Adult, and Counselor Education at East Carolina University. Alison is completing both the Clinical Mental Health Counseling and Student Affairs and College Counseling specializations. Alison aims to work in a university counseling center after pursuing a doctoral degree.

Beth is also completing both the Clinical Mental Health Counseling and Student Affairs and College Counseling specializations. Beth hopes to pursue a doctoral degree followed by a career as a professor as well as practicing as a family counselor.

Chapter 12

Setting Group Norms

James M. Benshoff and Adria E. Shipp

Goals and Learning Objectives:

1. Create a common set of flexible group ---norms to guide group members' behavior and interactions in group.
2. Increase group members' self-awareness as they reflect on individual participation in the process of setting group norms.
3. Build group cohesion.

Appropriate Course(s): Introduction to Counseling, Helping Relationships, Social and Cultural Counseling

Point in Group When Activity is Used: This activity can be helpful when conducted early in a class/group. Group norm setting is appropriate for many types of groups in a variety of settings and can set the tone for a class/group if done at the beginning.

Estimated Time Length: This activity can be completed within a 40-50 minute time frame. More time will be needed for larger groups.

1. 5-10 minutes: Individual brainstorming time for each group member to develop his/her list of group norms. Each member will develop his/her list of group norms.

2. 5-10 minutes: Collectively organizing and coming to consensus on a final list of group norms. All group members will organize and reach consensus on a final list of group norms.

3. 20-30 minutes: Processing and reflecting upon the experience of creating group norms and reaching consensus.

Technology and/or Materials Needed: Materials needed may vary depending on the online platform being used to collect individual and group information. For example a Discussion Board or a Wiki would offer a simple, asynchronous way to collect individual responses and provide an online environment for group members to discuss their ideas and brainstorm together. Ideally, there also would be a synchronous component (e.g., instant messaging, video messaging, online white board, Elluminate/Collaborate) to allow group members to communicate in real time to do the work of consensus building. Processing and reflecting also could take place online using one of the above mentioned platforms.

A Wiki is a website that allows the creating and editing of a number of web pages. This allows for the sharing and editing of information among a number of users.

Directions for Activity: Details in these directions (indicated by [ ]) can change depending on specifics of task given to group members. Also, directions may need to be modified depending on whether the activity is done in a synchronous or asynchronous format. Directions below are for a <u>synchronous</u> group environment.

Step 1: *"What do you think the [3] most important [rules/expectations] should be for our group? Working on your own, take 5–10 minutes to make a list of the [3] [rules/expectations] you think will be most important for us to follow as we work together. You can create your list in the text box, but please wait to post (by hitting the Enter key) in the chat window until we give you the instruction to post."* The number of rules/expectations you ask them to post will depend on the number of group members and size of the display in which they will post.

Step 2: *"Everyone ready? OK, go ahead and post your list."* All group members post their list of group norms in the chat box online, making them visible to all group members

Step 3: The instructor organizes and posts all responses on the online whiteboard for all group members to view. *"Now, look at everyone else's choices. What differences and similarities do you notice? The next step is for you all to agree on a master list of the [3] most important [rules/expectations] for our group. So, take the next [5–10 minutes] to talk about this and develop the master list for the group."* Group members can collaborate using chat while the instructor organizes the discussion on the online whiteboard.

Step 4: *"So, is each of you comfortable with the master list you came up with? How did the group go about the process of making decisions about what [rules/expectations] will be most important for our group? Who had leadership roles in helping the process along?"*

Discussion/Processing Questions:

1. How did you decide, as a group, which group norms would be on the final list?
2. What was your role in creating the final list of group norms?
3. How do you think your role in this activity might have been different in a face-to-face situation?
4. How did your group work together to accomplish the task?
5. What helped or hindered your group's ability to complete the task?
6. What did you learn about other class/group members through this activity?
7. What did you learn about yourself?

8. How will you apply what you've learned about others or yourself as we work together in this class/group?

Potential Adaptations: This activity can be adapted to include other types of consensus-building activities depending on the topic/focus of the group.

Cautions/Potential Issues: It is helpful if group members are unable to see others' responses until after deciding on their own list. This helps maintain the uniqueness of each group member's responses.

Contributing Author(s):

Dr. James Benshoff is a professor in the Department of Counseling and Educational Development at the University of North Carolina at Greensboro. He is a convert to experiential learning, and enjoys the challenging of introducing creative ideas and teaching methods in his graduate courses. One of his primary areas of interest is group process and leadership.

Dr. Adria Shipp is a licensed school counselor currently working as School Health Program Manager with Piedmont Health Services in Alamance County, North Carolina. She also teaches hybrid courses for the Department of Counselor Education and Supervision at The University of Northern Colorado in Greeley, CO. She is especially interested in using online and mobile technology to enhance existing counselor educational practices.

Chapter 13

The Dimensions of Diversity

Steven W. Schmidt

Goals and Learning Objectives:

1. Help students to examine the dimensions of diversity in a holistic way
2. Allow students to reflect and assess their own dimensions of diversity
3. Build group cohesion and facilitate interaction by providing a mechanism for students to share information about themselves

Appropriate Course(s): Social and Cultural Counseling, and potentially any course that emphasizes a better understanding of the dimensions of diversity.

Point in Group When Activity is Used: This activity is best used toward the beginning of a course or unit, when students are getting to know their colleagues in class. It is also a good way to introduce the concept of diversity in course units (and may be used at the start or end of those units).

Estimated Time Length: This activity could be run during the duration of an online unit. It should be run over the timespan of several days of an online course, in order to give participants time to participate, reflect, and respond. Time spent on this activity could depend on participants involved. It could take anywhere from 20 to 50 minutes (over the course of a unit). This is assuming students will participate between 3-5 times in a back-and-forth exchange.

Technology and/or Materials Needed: An online discussion forum, whereby students can post content and respond to people who respond to their postings, is necessary for this activity to work (i.e., Blackboard, Moodle, D2L).

It is also important that students participate in this activity with the understanding of diversity on a broad level. This definition of diversity, from the University of California Berkeley website is a good one to serve as a basis for this activity: "Diversity refers to human qualities that are different from our own and those of groups to which we belong; but that are manifested in other individuals and groups. Dimensions of diversity include (but are not limited to): age, ethnicity, gender, physical abilities/qualities, race, sexual orientation, educational background, geographic location, income, marital status, military experience, parental status, religious beliefs, work experience, and job classification" (Source: University of California Berkeley. http://hrweb.berkeley.edu/diversity/why-diversity)

Directions for Activity: Students are divided up into groups of two or three. Each student should post some examples of how he or she is diverse. These postings can be in the form of written descriptions, video clips, photos, or any combination thereof (the content of the postings should be easily understood by the other students). The other students then respond to that initial posting by discussing ways in which they are both similar and different than the first student. This way, students can see what they have in common with their colleagues and what is different among them. They might also discuss the following:

1. Which dimensions of diversity are most visible? Least visible?
2. Which dimensions of diversity are easiest or hardest (in different situations)? What obstacles or roadblocks do people of certain dimensions of diversity have to face?
3. Which dimensions of diversity do you consider most often in yourself? Least often?
4. Are there ways in which you are diverse that you had not considered before this activity? If so, what were they?
5. Which dimensions of diversity each student has most knowledge about or experience with (and least knowledge and experience).

Discussion/Processing Questions:

1. What did you learn about your classmates?
2. What did you learn about yourself?
3. How has your understanding of the concept of diversity changed as a result of this activity?
4. What did you learn about specific dimensions of diversity that you did not know in the past, or had not considered?

In addition to these questions, the questions noted in the "Directions for Activity" could be discussed after the activity.
Longer term follow-up could also be done. If this activity is done at the beginning of a course, follow up might occur toward the end of the course, to discuss what participants learned about each other, and about diversity, in general. Learners might reflect on how this learning influences their counseling practice (or could influence their practice, going forward).

Potential Adaptations: This activity could be done using many different forms of technology. For example, students could post video clips on YouTube. They could develop their own wikis or blogs, as well. Students might also consider developing their own web pages. Most of the above allow for others to comment on the original poster's (student's) work, which is key in this exercise.

Cautions/Potential Issues: Students do not have to share all dimensions of their own diversity if they do not wish to. They can select what they want to share. Students should not feel forced to reveal specific dimensions of their own diversity if they are uncomfortable doing so.

Contributing Author: Dr. Steven W. Schmidt is an Associate Professor of Adult Education in the Department of Higher, Adult, and Counselor Education at East Carolina University. His research interests include cultural competence, workplace training and development, and online teaching and learning.

ACTIVITIES for

GROUP

COUNSELING

Chapter 14

Theoretical Integration

Aaron H. Oberman

Goals and Learning Objectives: The purpose of this activity is to help students develop their own unique theoretical orientation by using images to construct the different elements that make-up components of their counseling theory.

The goals for this activity include:

1. Help students to process how the many components of the counseling theories combine to create their own unique theoretical orientation.
2. Engage the students by using icons to represent different aspects of their own theoretical orientation.
3. Aid students in reflecting about the different components that make-up each of the counseling theories.

Appropriate Course(s): This activity is designed for use in Counseling Theories; however, the activity can be modified to fit into many of the core counseling classes, including Group Counseling.

Point in Group When Activity is Used: Because the activity is focused on theory, it would go well at the end of the Counseling Theories or Group Counseling class (after gaining sufficient knowledge regarding various theories) to get students thinking about what theories they might use in group work as well as with individual counseling.

Estimated Time Length: 90 minutes

Technology and/or Materials Needed: Access to a computer with Internet access.

Directions for Activity:

1. Explain to the students that they will be completing an online collage that represents their theoretical orientation. Creating a sample to show students would be helpful so they clearly understand the assignment expectations (see Sample Collage).

2. This collage will contain a minimum of 10 icons that represent each student's core counseling beliefs about working with clients. Also inform students that the collages will be presented later on to other class members.
3. Instruct the students to open up one Microsoft PowerPoint slide, and type their first name in the middle of the page.
4. Next, ask the students to open the website www.google.com and click on the images tab (or another site with images).
5. Give the students 30-45 minutes to surf the World Wide Web to locate, copy, and paste images into the collage.
6. As the students finish, have each student video themselves explaining the various parts of the collage, with a limit of approximately 5 minutes. Once students have videoed themselves, have each student upload his or her video to YouTube and post a copy of the link to your course site, such as Blackboard.
7. After students have posted their videos, students may view each collage and respond to what was seen.

Discussion/Processing Questions:

1. How do these images reflect your original thoughts about your counseling theory at the beginning and middle of the semester? Write down a few of your thoughts to compare with the images in your collage.
2. How did you feel when you were searching for images related to your theoretical orientation?
3. How did you go about selecting images to represent your theoretical orientation?
4. Were there any challenges for you in finding images for your collage?
5. On a scale of 1 to 10, how well do you feel this collage represents your theoretical orientation? What else would you have liked to include?

Potential Adaptations: A variety of platforms may be used to post and share videos and comments. In addition, students may list (in a few sentences) their core counseling beliefs at the beginning, middle, and end of class. This would allow them to review their lists at the various points in the course and compare them to the collage images to see if they match.

Cautions/Potential Issues: When sharing personal information there is some risk on the part of the students. Just be aware of this risk, regardless of how small, and work to create an environment that is safe and trusting.

Sample Collage:

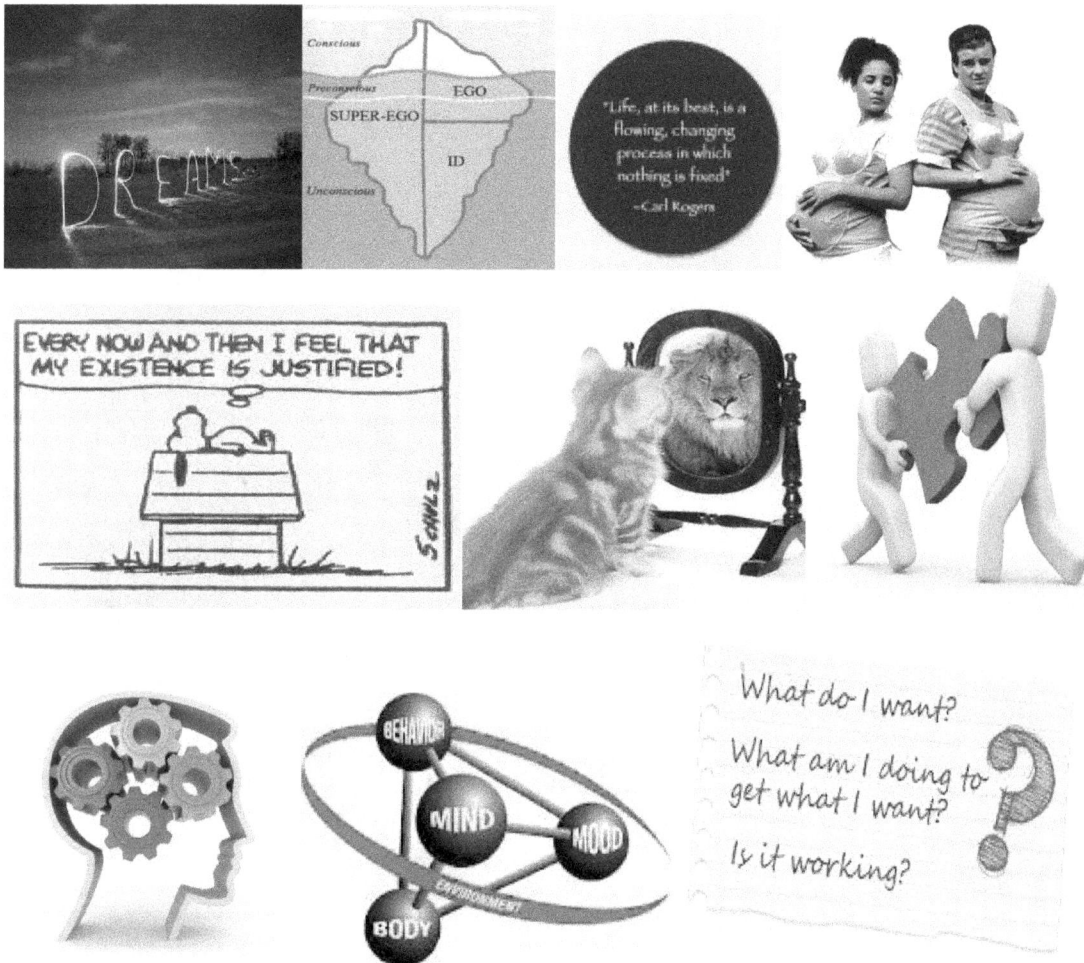

Contributing Author(s): Aaron H. Oberman, Ph.D., NCC is an associate professor of counselor education at The Citadel. He is also the coordinator of school counseling field experiences. His research interests are in the areas of supervision, job satisfaction, the ASCA Model, and technology.

Chapter 15

Picture Perfect

J. Scott Glass

Goals and Learning Objectives:

1. Engage in self-disclosure
2. Begin to imagine self free of presenting issues
3. Acknowledge issues and impact on personal situations
4. Use effective communication skills
5. Focus on own sense of self

Appropriate Course(s): Introduction to Counseling and Group Counseling

Point in Group When Activity is Used: This activity can be used at any time when self-disclosure and self-reflection is desired. Typically this activity has been implemented earlier in a class in an effort to build some rapport among members of the group. The risk of self-disclosure may be minimized as much as instructor deems necessary, making the activity relatively safe for participants.

Estimated Time Length: The time of this activity depends on the level of creativity that is desired. As the instructor, I want my students to have the freedom to express themselves as genuinely and creatively as possible, so I would allow at least a couple of hours for group members to create their "posters."

Technology and/or Materials Needed: Access to computers and the internet, specifically Glogster (http://www.glogster.com). Glogster is a website that allows users to create expressive, personalized virtual posters. It is a way to use graphics, photos, videos, music and text to create "Glogs," or personal representations for individuals or groups. It is a free program which requires users to create a free account. Glogs can then be shared via the web, Blackboard, Facebook, MySpace, etc.

Directions for Activity: Group members are asked to recognize the impact of their presenting issues on their current lives. Each student is asked to create and share one virtual poster representing both their "issue" and how they might picture themselves if this issue were no longer

94

impacting them in a negative way. In doing so, members may also identify how they view the issue and impediments they see in trying to deal effectively with the situation. All of this information is included on a single Glog.

Inform the group that you want them to picture themselves and their lives if they were to be free of an "issue" that is troubling them. Specific directions may include the following:

For this activity, I want you to "Picture Yourselves Perfect." You are being asked to create a virtual poster of yourselves that represents yourself and the issue or issues that bring you to counseling, as well as shows how you might see yourself if you were free of the issue or issues that have caused you to be a member of this group. How might you be different? What keeps you from making these desired changes? What stands in the way of how things are today and how you would like things to be? You are being given the freedom to be as creative as possible, but do recognize that you will be asked to share your posters with the other group members.

For this activity, you will use a program called Glogster EDU (http://edu.glogster.com) to create your poster. This is a free program, but you will need to open an account by creating a log in name and password. There is no charge for this process. Once you have created your account you may begin to create your poster.

First, I want you to identify the issue or issues that brought you to counseling and think about how it has impacted your life. Next, I want you to picture yourself perfect. On your poster you may include a variety of items including pictures, videos, music, text and more. Your task is to create this poster to represent how you might see yourself differently if your presenting issue was not such a factor in your life. You may use any and all forms of presentation on your posters. Represent what you believe your issue is, how you would like for it to be, and what you see as roadblocks that keep you from realizing your "Picture Perfect" selves.

Upon completion of your poster, you will share the final product with the group, as well as view those posters created by other group members.

Once posters are completed, group members may share the link to their posters via email, Blackboard threads, etc., and discussions may then be held via email threads or chats through discussion boards or group blogs.

Discussion/Processing Questions:
1. Was it difficult to decide how to represent your issue on the poster? Why or why not?
2. How did it feel to create a visual representation of your presenting issue?
3. Now that you have created a visual representation of what keeps you from effectively dealing with this issue, how might you go about developing strategies for addressing it?

4. After viewing the posters of other group members, how does it make you feel about your own personal struggles in relation to the group as a whole?

Potential Adaptations: In order to lessen the anxiety related to sharing such personal posters, group members could be paired with one other group member and posters could be shared and discussed between two people as opposed to being shared with the entire group. This could strengthen personal connections and increase meaningful dialogue between small groups.

Cautions/Potential Issues: It is important to recognize that this activity does require risk on the part of the participants. It may be difficult for some group members to openly acknowledge personal issues and make them more "real" by creating a visual representation. Depending on the stage of the group/class, this activity may be very in-depth or may remain somewhat simplistic. Students should be encouraged and applauded for various levels of disclosure that may be expressed.

Brief Description of Contributing Author(s): Dr. J. Scott Glass is an Associate Professor in the Department of Higher, Adult and Counselor Education at East Carolina University. His research interests include adventure based counseling, group processing, and issues related to group counseling.

Chapter 16

Examining Group Stage, Content, and Process

Lorraine J. Guth

Goals and Learning Objectives:

1. Participants will increase their understanding of group stage, content, and process concepts
2. Participants will conceptualize the stage, content, and process interactions of their online learning group

Appropriate Course(s): Group Work

Point in Group When Activity is Used: This activity should be used at the beginning, middle, and end of the online class.

Estimated Time Length: Each time the activity is done it will take 45-60 minutes for each participant in the online environment. Total time for the activity to be completed for the entire group will depend on deadlines set by facilitator.

Technology and/or Materials Needed: The activity is best facilitated in a Course Management System (CMS), Learning Management System (LMS), or Virtual Learning Environment (VLE) that has a discussion board or forum capability. This would allow participants and the facilitator to post comments and share ideas. In addition, textbooks or reading materials that explain the group stage, content, and process concepts are needed (See for example, Jacobs, Masson, Harvill, & Schimmel, 2012; Corey, Corey, & Corey, 2010; Hulse-Killacky, Killacky, & Donigian, 2001; Gladding, 2008).

Directions for Activity:

Discussion/Processing Questions:

- What themes did you notice regarding group stage, group content, or group process of this online learning group?
- If the class is not in a working stage, what would help to move the class into this stage?
- If you did this activity previously in this course, what changes have you noticed in this online learning group regarding stage, content, and process considerations?

- What feelings emerged for you during the activity?
- What thoughts did you have as you engaged in the activity?
- What have you learned from the activity?

Potential Adaptations: Appropriately adapted computer equipment or assistive technology may be needed for some participants who have disabilities.

Cautions/Potential Issues: It is important to establish the norms listed at the beginning of this activity related to confidentiality, respect, and acceptance. Care must be taken to appropriately process any issues that surface in the discussion board posts and to reinforce the norms that were set at the beginning of the online course.

Credits/References:

Blumenfeld, W. J. (1993). *Homophobia: How we all pay the price.* Boston: Beacon Press.

Corey, M. S., Corey, G., & Corey, C. (2010). *Groups: Process and practice* (7th ed.). Belmont, CA: Brooks/Cole.

Gladding, S. (2008). *Groups: A counseling specialty* (5th ed.). Upper Saddle River, NJ: Merrill/Prentice Hall.

Hulse-Killacky, Killacky, J., & Donigian, J. (2001). *Making task groups work in your world.* Upper Saddle River, NJ: Merrill/Prentice Hall.

Jacobs, E. E., Masson, R. L., Harvill, R. L., & Schimmel, C. J. (2012). *Group counseling: Strategies and skills* (7th ed.). Belmont, CA: Brooks/Cole.

Contributing Author(s): Lorraine J. Guth, Ph.D., is a Professor in the Department of Counseling, Indiana University of Pennsylvania. She teaches multicultural and diversity issues, group counseling, and group practicum courses for graduate counseling students. She has led or co-led a variety of counseling, personal growth, and psychoeducational groups. She has conducted numerous presentations on group work and recently presented on group work at the National Board of Certified Counselors International Counseling Conference in Thimphu, Bhutan. She has also published several articles on group work and serves on the Association for Specialists in Group Work Leadership team as the Awards Committee co-chair.

Chapter 17

The Sharing of Selves to Promote Group Interaction

Graham Disque and J. Logan Tindell

Goals and Learning Objectives:

1. Decrease predisposed fears and anxieties related to participating in group work
2. Build connections with other group members by asking participants to share various parts of themselves
3. Model how to address similarities and differences with other group members in appropriate ways
4. Increase communication and compassion within the group
5. Have participants recognize and respect different points of views

Appropriate Course(s): Human Relations and Group Counseling

Point in Group When Activity is Used: This activity is best used at the beginning of a group to move the members into making contact with each other in a safe way. The exercise can also be used at various times when particular patterns of interaction are redundant or over identification with a particular role is taking place in the group. This activity can be implemented more than once with the first exposure serving as an informative session as group members are asked to speak from predetermined parts. The subsequent sessions should encourage the members of the group to be more aware of their own over developed and under developed parts.

Estimated Time Length: This activity should be conducted within a 1-3 hour time frame which will include time to process students' thoughts, emotions, and concerns after participation in the activity.

Technology and/or Materials Needed: Access to a computer with online chat room or Skype capabilities is necessary for utilization of activity. Accessibility to chat rooms would allow the instructor to view the conversations of the group members in real time which would ensure that the activity is done correctly and by facilitation could be provided as necessary. The use of these technological programs would create a live "in the moment" session so that spontaneity would be present.

Directions for Activity: Students are randomly assigned a specific role for the activity. The following are some of the roles/personalities that are frequently seen within groups. These roles, along with their definitions, may include the following:

The caretaker/helper/rescuer: Characterized by the part looking for opportunities to uplift others and thus sacrifices himself/herself, their self-worth is contingent on the ability to help others

The pusher: Characterized by always looking toward the future, wants things to be better, and believes anything can be solved with effort

The peacekeeper: Can be seen as always avoiding conflict perceiving it as dangerous and finds it hard to see conflict between others without intervening

The victim: Always looking for injustice towards them, wants empathy and understanding from others but is not expecting to get it

The blamer: Often serves a purpose for the group as a whole by allowing the group to transfer common feelings onto this blaming part, allowing the group to experience own concerns

The troublemaker-instigator: Seen as annoying and will not let sleeping dogs lie

The cheerleader: Constantly giving encouragement to other group members

The spiritual guide: Turns the concerns of the group into a spiritual dimension with statements such as, "It's God's will, let me tell you a Zen story"

The inner critic: Presents everything wrong with him/herself, is self-defeating, and internalizes everything negatively

The vulnerable: Often shy, skittish, avoidant, and easily hurt

The bully: Uses threats to manipulate or control to maintain a sense of power

The disenfranchised: Powerless, perceives that there are not options, does not feel valued, feels prejudiced against

The privileged: Expects that the world will always revolve around him/her, feels like people should always validate him/her

The patriarch: Controls and limits anything that is perceived to be feminine

The psychological researcher/knower: Super reasonable, always relying on research and statistics to back up whatever he/she is saying.

Once students are assigned their roles they are asked to remain in that role during the whole exercise and not reveal the name of their role to the other participants. The assigned roles can also be portrayed by different genders, ages, races, and sexual orientations. For example, a male member who is 22 may be assigned the vulnerable role that is a lesbian who is 50 years old. Some roles may be more submissive or dominate resulting in the person not talking as much during the session or taking over the session. It is important for the facilitator to manage the session without interrupting the natural persona of the various roles. This means that the student will speak directly for his/her specified role and the members of the group will respond from their own unique roles. The facilitator can check with each participant before beginning by asking, "Do you understand the role that you have been given?," or, "Are you able to speak for that role in this group?"

Once participants are clear about their assigned roles they will view a scenario created by the facilitator. The facilitator will pick one group member to play the character outlined in the scenario. This member will improvise the responses to the other group members who are playing various roles. In a more advanced stage of the group the scenario can come from a participant's actual experience. Here are a couple of examples of possible scenarios:

1. *A woman's grandfather is dying. She feels guilty and ashamed over the lack of contact she has had with him. She also feels some relief that he might be dying because of his abusive ways in the past and hardship he created for members of the family. She is confused by her conflicted feelings of love and anger.*

With the scenario established, the group is now open for discussion. The participants then respond from their different roles to the group member who shared the scenario. This discussion will either flow naturally or be guided by the facilitator. The blamer role, for example may say something like, "I had someone in my life that died before I could tell them how I felt and I still regret it to this day I think you will too." Or they might say, "It sounds to me as if you're just being nice to them now and giving in to them because they are dying." A rescuer/helper part may be pulled into the conversation and tell the blamer "I can't believe you said that, this person needs your sympathy not your judgment (turning attention back to the scenario player). How can I help you feel better? That must be really hard."

2. *A young man informs the group that his girlfriend of two years has just broken up with him and he is feeling depressed. He didn't see it coming and doesn't understand why she is leaving. He suspects she has been lying to him and using him all along and thinks she is moving on as if he never existed. A victim role might identify with him and share, "I had a girlfriend too. I treated her like a queen and she still broke up with me!" The patriarch role may see this as an opportunity to throw gas on the fire while the spiritual role may try to point out that it just wasn't meant to be and that all things have a purpose and work out in the end and the psychological knower concludes with statistics about how long relationships last and ten ways to avoid common pitfalls.*

As the discussion concludes, the members can guess at the identities of the parts that were being played and reveal what they were playing.

Discussion/Processing Questions:

1. How was it to speak using this role?
2. Were you experiencing any sensations within your body or changes in body posture as you were acting out your given personality?
3. Did you find it difficult to remain in the role that was assigned to you? If yes, what made it difficult?
4. Did one member of the group in particular make it harder for you to stay in your role? Why or why not?
5. Can you give an example of experiencing these roles in real life? When and with whom do these roles tend to come out?
6. If this role were to come out more or less frequently in your daily interactions, how might your life be different?
7. Which of these personalities do you exhibit the most? Which of these personalities do you exhibit the least?
8. If you could use this group to develop an underdeveloped role, what role would that be?

Potential Adaptations: Possible considerations for students with disabilities would include using software to convert speech to text via microphone for those students who have decreased motor functioning, as well as for students who have complications with language formation.

Cautions/Potential Issues: One issue to consider when implementing this exercise is that lack of face to face contact can result in loss of nonverbal information which could otherwise heighten the experience of the activity. Information reflecting emotions of anxiety, anger, or fear could be lost. One technological issue to consider would be that in the case that the chat room is too crowded, a delay in response time from the members of the group may occur. When using Skype one consideration would be possible time delays of speech patterns making facial expressions out of sync.

　　As with any therapy session or learning experience in class, moments of psychological distress could arise within the members. This could happen in this exercise due to certain assigned roles triggering suppressed feelings. In light of this the group member has the right to veto any assigned role he or she is not truly comfortable experiencing. It would be helpful for the facilitator to ask physiological questions to gauge heart rate, breathing rate, or tightness in specific areas of the body if distress is suspected of occurring.

Credits/References: This exercise has been influenced by the ideas presented in the work of Richard Schwartz on Internal Family Systems and the work of Hal and Sidra Stone on Voice Dialogue.

Contributing Author(s): Dr. Graham Disque is a Professor of Counseling at East Tennessee State University. He has over 20 years experience teaching and leading groups. He is an approved supervisor through the American Association of Marriage and Family Therapy. His interests are in developing awareness and integrating the selves that emerge through relationships.

J. Logan Tindell is a Masters Candidate in Counseling at East Tennessee State University. He has co-facilitated groups dealing with issues of grief and divorce and also has led psycho educational groups to families and patients at an inpatient psychiatric hospital. His interests include Internal Family Systems Theory, Bowen Systems Theory, and Human Validation Model.

ACTIVITIES for LEGAL and ETHICAL ISSUES in COUNSELING

Chapter 18

Instagram: Professional Identity, Role Orientation, and

Ethical Knowledge Display

Melissa Luke

Goals and Learning Objectives:

1. Students will actively engage technology as part of their learning, as a means to express their professional identity, role orientation, and ethical knowledge.
2. Students' reflective practice will increase, thereby promoting their counseling development.
3. Students will use technology as a mechanism to meaningfully interact with one another.
4. Class cohesion and interpersonal caring will increase.

Appropriate Course(s):

This activity relates to Professional Identity, as well as that of Professional Orientation and Ethics. The activity was developed for and incorporated into an Introduction to Professional Counseling course.

Specific CACREP 2009 Standards Addressed:

Section II, Professional Identity, Knowledge G1b, G1c, G1h, G1i, and G1j.

KNOWLEDGE G.1. PROFESSIONAL ORIENTATION AND ETHICAL PRACTICE

Studies that provide an understanding of all of the following aspects of professional functioning:

b. professional roles, functions, and relationships with other human service providers,
including strategies for interagency/interorganization collaboration and communications;
c. counselors' roles and responsibilities as members of an interdisciplinary emergency
management response team during a local, regional, or national crisis, disaster or other
trauma-causing event;

h. the role and process of the professional counselor advocating on behalf of the
profession;
i. advocacy processes needed to address institutional and social barriers that impede
access, equity, and success for clients; and
j. ethical standards of professional organizations and credentialing bodies, and
applications of ethical and legal considerations in professional counseling.

Point in Group When Activity is Used:

This activity requires some professional knowledge, but lends itself to an ongoing or longitudinal implementation. Ideally, the activity permits a formative record of the students' development and not solely a representation of a summative experience. As such, it is possible to use this activity throughout an entire semester long course (e.g., requiring students to engage in a 'posting' and response once or twice per week). It is also feasible to impose time limits on the assignment duration (e.g., students required to engage in daily postings & responses for a period of 2-3 weeks). If the later format is used, the instructor may wish to increase the frequency of required postings so that the students have more practice in identifying, reflecting, and responding to their own and others' professional identity, role orientation, and ethical knowledge displays.

Instagram Technology:

Instagram is a free social networking media program that currently has100 million members (Meredith, 2012). Instagram members share photographs with other members within the network. The Instagram program allows members to take a photo, apply various filters, and then upload the photo with a description or caption. Other members can then view these photos, follow the user, as well as 'like' or comment upon the original photo.

Materials Needed:

For this activity, all students and the instructor need to download the free 'Instagram' application to their Android or iphone, ipad, web enabled ipod, or Mac computer. Additionally, access to a web enabled camera is also necessary, in order to take pictures that will be uploaded and shared across 'Instagram.' Although users can upload and access photos solely through 'Instagram,' the application also facilitates sharing via Facebook, Twitter, etc. Because the 'Instagram' application allows users to create multiple accounts, a 'closed' group can be set up for the purpose of this course activity.

Estimated time length:

Students will need to spend approximately 15 minutes with the initial downloading of the 'Instagram' application to their Android or iphone, ipad, web enabled ipod, Mac computer, and an additional 15 minutes to become familiar with the features of the program itself. Thereafter, the daily postings will require some forethought on the part of the student, but will take only a few minutes to upload. Following (reviewing) and then responding to the postings of classmates may involve more time, particularly when the class group is larger than 10. In such cases, students could be assigned to follow and respond to the posts of a select number of other students in the class, but this introduces subgroupings and even if rotated, can complicate group dynamics. The duration of the activity throughout the semester is determined by how long the instructor wishes to keep this communication continuing, ranging from a couple weeks to the entire 16-week semester.

Directions for Activity:

1. Instructor or group leader distributes assignment parameters, including directions related to the 'Instagram' technology and expectations for how frequently students are expected to post, as well as respond to others' uploaded photos.
   <u>Sample directions</u>: Over the next four weeks, you will be expected to participate in an Instagram assignment as part of your field experience. Each week, you are required to take and upload three different photographs (12 total over the duration of the assignment). Each week, one photo will reflect something about your *professional identity*, one will reflect something about your *professional role(s)*, and one will represent something about your understanding of *ethical knowledge*. The explicit subject of each photo is at your discretion, although it is imperative that you adhere to all legal mandates, ethical standards, and site related policies that apply to distribution of images. (Please be aware that when in doubt, you should seek clarification). To download the Instagram program, you will need to go to the iTunes App store or Google Play and follow the directions listed.

2. Information about how to select and share user names within a 'closed' group is distributed, including the fact that students can open a separate 'Instagram' account for any personal activity they wish.
   <u>Sample directions</u>: Once you have downloaded the Instragram program, you will be asked for a user name. For our class purposes, your user name will be your first and last initial followed by our course abbreviation. For example, mine will be MLCOU612. You will need to email me your exact user name, and after collecting

everyone's information, I will distribute to the class via email. Please keep this information handy, as this is how you will identify one another over the assignment.

If you already have an Instagram account under a different user name, you will need to create a second account under a separate email address with the above user name, as this is an account will be solely for student/professional purposes. Related, if you enjoy your class assignment and wish to create a second account for your personal use, you may certainly do so, however, you must keep all personal and student/professional use separate. Accordingly, you will need to denote this course related Instagram account as 'closed' meaning that only the class will be able to access your pictures for viewing and comments.

To do this, you need to go to "Edit Profile' and make sure that you have made this 'private.' Thereafter, only after you have received and agreed to classmates' requests to follow you, will they be able to access your material.

3. Instructor shares information about how to 'follow' classmates' posted photos, and directs students' attention to how they can double check whether they are following and being followed by all of the other classmates and instructor.

   Sample directions: Once you receive the email from me, listing each class member and their Instagram user name, you will be able to send requests to each person, asking to 'follow' them. To do this, you will need to go to the "explore' toolbar, second to left on the bottom of the screen, denoted by a compass star. Once you enter this, you will have the choice to explore by user or hashtag, and you will select user. When you enter and search by a classmate's user name, you will then be directed to making the request to follow. You will repeat this process for all 10 classmates and myself. Concurrently, you will be receiving similar requests from classmates and myself, to which you will respond affirmatively, permitting us to follow you. Although you will be able to identify each of us by the similar user name format, and you know that you will have a total of 10 followers for class, you can also double check any requests against the email listing.

4. Instructor or group leader shares his or her own user name, and displays a couple photos as examples of professional identity, role orientation, and ethical knowledge displays. Instructor may wish to provide some structure related to selection of user names, such as beginning first and last initial followed by course abbreviation (e.g., MLCOU612).

<u>Suggested directions:</u> The instructor can either pull up previously posted photographs on his or her Instragram account or provide examples via power point. In doing so, the instructor will want to provide at least one photograph and illustrative caption for each type of display required within the assignment, namely professional identity, professional roles, and ethical knowledge. Below are examples obtained via Google Images.

Within the professional identity example, the following photograph could be shared with a caption of 'Not the G word still!':

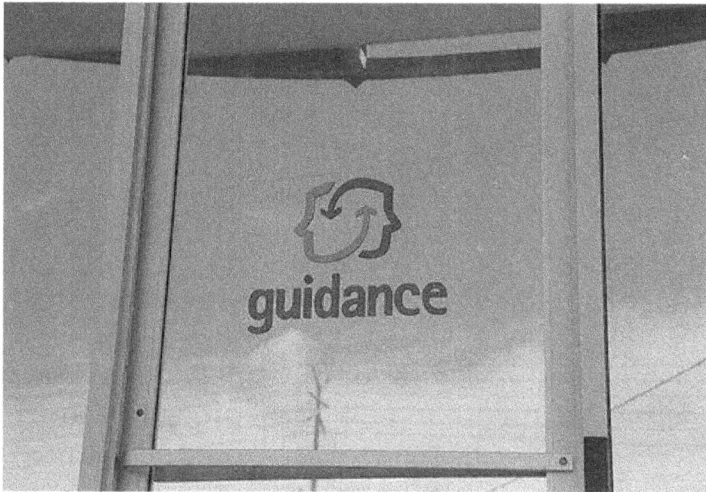

As a reflection of professional role(s), the following photograph could be offered with a caption of 'Some of my best work happens here:'

For ethcial knowledge display, the following might be shared with a caption of "Parental consent and Student Assent for photo sharing obtained:'

5. Once students have downloaded the 'Instagram' application and have become familiar with the technology, the professional identity, role orientation, and ethical knowledge displays begin. Instructor may wish to set a minimum or maximum number of uploaded images per day or week. For example, students might be asked to upload 3 photos a week, one that represents a professional identity image, another that symbolizes role orientation, and a third that reflects some aspect of ethical knowledge. Each photo would also be given a 'caption,' wherein students have opportunity to connect words to the image.
Suggested directions: After sharing the example images and captions in step 4, the instructor may wish to facilitate a discussion about technology, professionalism, and the potential for images and captions have the potential of doing more than fulfilling (or not) the aims of the assignment. This is an opportunity to review ACA and/or ASCA ethical standards, CACREP standards, and any other accreditation or professional standards (e.g., NCATE) on which the counseling students are evaluated.

6. Students are then also instructed about the requirements for responding to the uploaded photos of their classmates via 'Instagram.' As a 'follower' of another user, the uploaded photos are automatically accessible through one's account. Thus, a student simply needs to open the 'Instagram' application and s/he will be able to see any uploaded images of classmates. As such, the student has an opportunity to 'like' a particular posting and/or respond via the comment function.
Sample directions: In addition to the requirement to post 3 photos a week for the next four weeks, you are also expected to respond to your classmates' postings, much like you might on a discussion board

forum. Although you may do more that the requirements, you minimally need to 'like' three photos (of the 30 each week you will view) and be prepared to offer a rationale for your selection. Additionally, you will need to comment upon five different classmates' photos. Although the length of your comments is not mandated, you may wish to connect the material to class reading, discussion, or concepts that we are covering this semester.

7. Concurrently, using reflective journals submitted directly to the instructor, a discussion board wherein the entire class can view postings, or even via intermittent email, students are asked to reflect on their experiences with the assignment.
   <u>Suggested directions:</u> Instructors may wish to have students reflect on their awareness, knowledge, and skills throughout the process of the assignment in a journal or reflection paper. In the past, I have also asked students to provide process observations to one another via a class discussion board, which could include giving their rationales for the 'liked' photos each week.

Discussion/Processing Questions:

1. What was the process of using 'Instagram' as a professional identity, role orientation, and ethical knowledge display like for you this week?
2. How might your experiences with the activity/technology be similar to and different than your counselor development more broadly?
3. What did you notice about yourself in relation to individual classmates as well as the overall group via the assignment? Any connections that can be made to group processes, dynamics, or themes?
4. Describe how the photographs posted appear to reflect your/another student's professional identity, understanding of professional roles and responsibilities, and professional ethics. What inferences might be drawn from this form of communication?
5. What themes did you see this week in the 'Instagram' postings of you and your classmates? How do you understand this in the context of the course material? Your developmental level? Your group cohesion?
6. What did you learn about yourself as a professional through the assignment? What did you learn about others?
7. What did you learn related to the content of professional identify, role orientation, and ethical knowledge? What did you learn about the processes (technological and group interaction)? Lastly, how can any of this knowledge be useful in your current or future work as a counselor?

Potential Adaptations:

This activity can be particularly useful with students who have expressive and receptive language learning disabilities, as it does not solely rely upon linguistic means for reflection and communication, and instead involves visual representation as well. Additionally, given the activity does not take place in real time and instead occurs in analogue, students requiring additional time to process and plan can be easily accommodated. Moreover, students with hearing loss and those requiring TTD modifications are able to readily engage without additional supports. That said, students with visual disabilities and those who are blind may need added adaptations. These modifications can include software that permits description of the photos and can read the students' captions.

Cautions/Potential Issues:

It is expected that students will have varying degrees of familiarity with the technology necessary to complete this activity. Accordingly, the concept of parallel process (Parkh, Janson, & Singelton, 2012) is helpful to understand the relationship between students' development of the content (i.e., professional identity, role orientation, and ethical knowledge), and their confidence and efficacy with the processes involved in displaying them. It is also expected that the visual representations and symbolic expression incorporated in to this activity will provide different access to and expression of students' increasing knowledge, awareness, and skills. Processing this as well as students' reactions can be helpful. Lastly, students should be reminded that despite the range of privacy settings available through the 'Instagram' application, their postings should be considered public and therefore, neither confidentiality nor privacy apply in the typical fashion they might in other class/group activities.

Credits/References:

The following references may be consulted as support for the relationship between expressive activities and counselor personal/professional development.

Degges-White, S., & Davis, N. (2010). *Bringing the Arts to the Science of Counseling,* New   York, NY: Springer.

Meredith, L. (September 14, 2012). The Instagram community hits 100 million users. *TechNews Daily.*

Parikh S. B., Janson, C, & Singelton, T. (2012) Video journaling as a method of reflective practice. *Counselor Education and Supervision, 51,* 33-49.

Contributing Author(s):

Dr. Melissa Luke is an Assistant Professor and the Coordinator of School Counseling at Syracuse University. She has over 15 years experience as a group worker, with a particular interest in using experiential interventions with children and adolescents. She utilizes such techniques within group work in the counselor training context as well, recently developing an online school counseling class.

114

Chapter 19

Blogging for Engaged Discussion and Critical Reflection

Kaye B. Dotson

Goals and Learning Objectives:

1. Participants will be linked to students and colleagues for professional and personal support, establishing their on-line presence and identity
2. Participants will increase their self-awareness of collaborative abilities and counseling skills through reading and reflecting on the blog posts of others
3. Participants will improve effectiveness of communication in the online arena

Appropriate Course(s): Professional orientation and ethical practice; Helping Relationships

Point in Group When Activity is Used: This activity should be used at the beginning of the class when participants are getting to know each other and throughout the course to enable interaction, discussion, and reflection.

Estimated Time Length: It will take approximately 10-15 minutes per week for each participant in the online environment. Total time for the activity to be completed for the entire group will depend on the responses to and by members of the group.

Technology and/or Materials Needed: Blogging is based upon asynchronous e-learning; therefore students need not be online at the same time. The activity is easily facilitated through any of the available course management systems, for example Blackboard or other web-based course management system that has blogging capability. Additionally, numerous easily accessible web applications are available for blogging including Blogger, WordPress, Movable Type, and LiveJournal among others that allow greater opportunities for students to construct their own meaning-making out of their experiences and those of their peers.

Directions for Activity: Pre-service counselors require examples and discussions of ideas and behaviors, with opportunities for professional reflection on many topics beyond their personal experiences. In the academic setting it can be difficult to provide realistic activities and experiences to prepare future counselor for all the experiences they may face. Guided discussions, in an examination of the practices and reactions to experiences of peers, followed by critical thought and reflection can help prepare students for future professional roles. Blogging, a common practice among students can be effectively used for providing opportunities to discuss, reflect, and engage while expanding their own perspectives (Ray & Hocutt, 2006). Blogging offers a means to facilitate desired interaction, dialog and critical reflection among students about topics that may be unfamiliar, or even uncomfortable. This blog activity will provide an avenue to allow for on-going discussion and reflection encouraging multiple understandings on a range of topics.

Pre-service counselors will share, reflect and communicate professionally under the supervision of a trained counselor educator. They will respond to other students experiencing similar or different situations and circumstances using a weekly blog designed to support the development of a personally meaningful knowledge base. Examples of topics to be discussed may include information about professional engagement and involvement in professional organizations along with the more sensitive confidentiality issues and ethical considerations. Instructors will provide topics in addition to questions with specific required readings to guide students within the blogging experience. Possible topics may include North Carolina Board of Licensed Professional Counselor requirements and differences in those requirements; counseling skills and techniques; or counselor/client relationships for example. In each week's informal discussion of the topic, four reflective questions will be proposed. The resulting dialog may open doors to enhanced reflection by participants.

Discussion/Processing Questions:

To allow pre-service counselors place and opportunity to apply their understanding of each blog topic and to guide pre-service counselors in the process for enhanced reflection for the development of broader perspectives, the following questions, based upon research by Yost, Sentner, & Forlenza-Bailey (2000) will be addressed following discussion of applicable topics:

Instructors will lead with, "In consideration of this week's topic _____,"

1. Describe what you would do.
2. Inform us as to why it matters.
3. How did it come to be like this?
4. How could it be done differently?

Potential Adaptations: This activity can be adapted for use with other technology including wiki's, discussion boards, or online journaling tools.

Further, this activity can be applicable to courses for enhanced discussion of cultural diversity, human growth and development, career development or other core curricular areas.

Cautions/Potential Issues: Instructors are encouraged to guide students in ethical digital citizenship in a proactive manner. It is important to discuss privacy and confidentiality issues at the beginning of this activity. Close monitoring by an experienced educator is essential to provide direction and a framework for topics.

Credits/References:

Ray, B. & Hocutt, M. (2006 Teacher created, teacher-centered Weblogs: Perceptions and practices. *Journal of Computing in Teacher Education, 23* (1), 11-18.

Yost, D.S., Sentner, S.M., & Forlenza-Bailey, A. (2000). An examination of the construct of critical reflection: Implications for teacher education programming in the 21st century. *Journal of Teacher Education, 51,* 39-49.

Contributing Author(s): Dr. Kaye B. Dotson is an Assistant Professor in the Department of Library Science at East Carolina University. Her area of research expertise is leadership development, particularly focused on skill development through practical, hands-on experiences. Her goals include ongoing examination to inspire innovative teaching and learning experiences; facilitation of training for educators within the online learning environment; and development of educators as change agents and leaders within schools.

118

Chapter 20

Legal Clips

Laurie Williamson

Goals and Learning Objectives:

1. Increase their self-awareness of their personal values and biases (Self-awareness)
2. Gain knowledge of legal and ethical guidelines relevant to the school setting (Content)
3. Gain knowledge of legal statutes influencing professional school counseling practice (Content)
4. Develop critical thinking skills and an ethical decision making processes (Decision Making)
5. Identify programs, policies, and procedures that will encourage primary prevention in the schools (Prevention)

Appropriate Course(s): Legal and Ethical Issues in Professional School Counseling

Point in Group When Activity is Used: Activity is to be implemented during entire length of the course.

Estimated Time Length: In-class discussions will identify the highlights from the week's on-line listserv postings and forum comments and question exchange. Time will vary with the intensity of the topic and how easily the instructor can segue into specific course and class objectives.

Technology and/or Materials Needed: An online course platform such as Blackboard, or other online opportunities for discussion boards or chat rooms.

Directions for Activity: In this course we are scheduled to meet face-to-face every other week. One course requirement is to subscribe to the *Legal Clips* listserv which is a service of the National School Boards Association's Office of General Counsel and the NSBA Council of School Attorneys (COSA). Students are required to review the week's case postings and engage in an on-line discussion regarding one or more of the legal cases. Students are generally very adept at this mode of communication. (I monitor the discussion threads regularly and comment, question, or clarify as warranted.)

Discussion/Processing Questions:

Questions will vary depending on the nature of the case being discussed, but here are some examples of questions that may be asked:

1. What is your initial reaction to this case? (Self-awareness)
2. Do you have any personal bias regarding this case? (Self-awareness)
3. Who are the stakeholders in this case? (Content)
4. What legal precedents have been established on this topic and may be used to determine the outcome of the case? (Content)
5. What ethical guidelines are involved? (Content)
6. What are the school counselor's roles and responsibilities in this case? (Content)
7. How might you respond to this situation? (Decision Making)
8. What are the possible outcomes/consequences to your response? (Decision Making)
9. What can be learned from this case? (Prevention/Preparation)
10. What type of proactive or preventative measures would you recommend in this case? (Prevention)
11. How might you impact your school's policies and procedures regarding the issues identified in this case? (Prevention)

Potential Adaptations: This activity should not pose any particular difficulty not already addressed by general academic accommodations (i.e., enhanced visual/audio technology equipment).

Cautions/Potential Issues: This listserv is an excellent addition to any legal and ethical course in counseling and provides students with real-life, real-time legal proceedings affecting education. As with any discussion of emotionally charged issues, students are reminded to be respectful of differing perspectives.

Credits/References: Legal Clips site as a service of the National School Boards Association's Office of General Counsel and the NSBA Council of School Attorneys (COSA). Access is found at http://legalclips.nsba.org.

Contributing Author(s): Dr. Laurie L. Williamson is a Professor in the Professional School Counseling program at Appalachian State University. She facilitates her courses as large group experiences and encourages lively discussion and debate of the issues.

ACTIVITIES for CLINICAL EXPERIENCES

Chapter 21

Reflecting Team Exercise for Skill Building

Leah K. Clarke

Goals and Learning Objectives:
1. Improve students' case conceptualization skills
2. Students gain self-awareness of how each experiences feedback on counseling skills
3. Identify counseling skills students wish to improve or gain
4. Students identify appropriate interventions they can implement in field experience work

Appropriate Course(s): Field Experiences

Point in Group When Activity is Used: Middle of course when students have had time to establish relationships with clients and build group cohesion with each other.

Estimated Time Length: 1 to 1.5 hours

Technology and/or Materials Needed:
Required for Instructor and Students: Secure video conferencing platform with related hardware (webcam, microphone, and speakers). This would be for the actual "meeting" in which the skills are reviewed and the activity is conducted. The author's institution uses OnSync's conferencing platform.
Recommended: Headsets with microphones to reduce feedback and static during video conference.
Alternate Technology: Option 1: In the absence of video conferencing technology, this activity could be conducted via a secure chat room, which is often available through a learning management system. Option 2: If the activity is to be conducted outside of class time or without the instructor present, the ability to record the video conference or chat is helpful so the instructor may view it after the fact. Option 3: If the instructor wishes to have the group view recordings of classmates' counseling skills, students would need hardware and software to create audio and video files of their work with clients, primarily a digital recording device. Also needed is a learning management platform (Blackboard, Sakai, etc.) to which video or audio files can be uploaded and shared. Privacy limitations may apply, instructors should work with their educational technology support to determine the level of privacy that can be achieved with their software and

clients should be informed when session recordings will be shared electronically.

Directions for Activity:
Preparation:
1. The instructor creates a group of 4-6 students.
2. A meeting time and date are chosen and communicated to all members
3. A video conference "room" or "meeting" is created by the instructor and access provided to all group members.
4. One student is chosen as the presenter
5. Prior to the meeting the chosen student selects a client to present. The instructor can provide guidance on a type of client, such as a client for whom they are having trouble identifying a diagnosis or a client with whom they are experiencing countertransference.
6. The student prepares the presentation and possibly an audio/video clip and submits them to the instructor. It is recommended that instructors provide criteria for what the student should include in the presentation, and the student should at least identify areas he or she wishes to improve or specific types of feedback he or she may desire. Case presentation guidelines (see below) were designed to address some specific CACREP skill-based standards.

Guidelines for Case Presentation I

Prior to group supervision, you should organize the following information about your client and your experiences with him/her. Write a summary of the information outlined below (perhaps in PowerPoint format). This should be sent to the instructor 24 hours before group supervision. If possible, please also submit a brief audio/video presentation of the chosen session of at least **10 minutes.** *Your introduction and review of the audio/video should last no more than* **30 minutes.** *This leaves the majority of the time for feedback and comments from your peers and supervisor.* **PLEASE REMEMBER TO MAINTAIN THE CONFIDENTIALITY OF YOUR CLIENTS BY NOT WRITING ANY INFORMATION THAT WOULD IDENTIFY THEM SPECIFICALLY.** *Your case presentation should include the following information:*

A.   *Personal data about client*
- *age, race, and gender*
- *cultural and diversity considerations*
- *family information/background*
- *social network & supports*
- *educational/employment information*
- *how client presents him/herself*
- *general impressions of the client*
- *client's strengths and level of functioning*

- *presenting concerns including 5–axis DSM diagnosis*
B. *Summarize counseling history of the client*
  - *what led the client to seek counseling at this time?*
  - *number of sessions with this client*
  - *briefly describe your approach to working with this client*
  - *accomplishments to date*
  - *any complicating factors*
  - *theoretical techniques used*
  - *auxiliary supports appropriate for client (referrals you have made or are considering making)*
  - *description of your relationship with client and including the impact of any similarities and differences between you and client that are notable (particularly consider culture, gender, class, language, disabilities)*
C. *Solicit feedback*

  - *what particular difficulties are you having with this case?*
  - *what kind of help/feedback would you like from this group?*

7. The instructor reviews the presentation to make sure that the student adequately protected the privacy of the client (e.g., names and identifying information removed; appropriate informed consent documents if filmed or recorded, etc.).

8. If using a recording to demonstrate work with a client, just before the group meeting the instructor should make the student's recording available to other students within the learning management system. It is not recommended that the instructor uploads the recording to the video conference platform.

At Time of Meeting:

1. All group members and the instructor log on to the video conference room. In the video conference format that the author uses, students may log in but not broadcast themselves with audio and video. When they are not broadcasting they can still write messages for the group to see in a chat box.

2. A welcoming tone is set with students and the instructor posting written greetings to each other. It is good for the instructor to begin broadcasting immediately as it is easier to lead verbally than with chat and gives the session a visual focus. The instructor can then continue to set the welcoming tone by doing a friendly check-in (i.e., did anyone get to do some self-care over fall break?) or highlighting accomplishments of student (i.e., Nigel and Jamie just finished taking the NCE- congratulations!). Keeping the energy and engagement levels high in an online setting can be challenging- the instructor needs to be a model.

3. The instructor should introduce the reflecting team process and discuss the rationale for using it. It can be initially uncomfortable for

group members to talk about the presenter's work without the presenter being able to respond directly. To address this I often emphasize that this process gives the presenter time and cognitive space to absorb the feedback without feeling they have to give answers or defend their work.

4. Prior to the student presentation, the instructor assigns roles or perspectives to the other group members from which they will consider and discuss the presenter's work. Alternately, the instructor could provide a list of roles and the students could choose. Borders and Brown (2005) provide an overview of options for these roles that can be used in group supervision. To determine which type of roles might be helpful the instructor can review the case presentation materials ahead of time, including what kind of feedback the presenter is looking for. Two options I prefer are:

   a. Each group member besides the presenter takes on a character perspective from which he or she will consider the session/client. Perspectives would include the client, the counselor, an important family member of the client, a theorist (Beck, Rogers, etc.), an experienced counselor/supervisor. This is a good option for when the focus is on the relationship between the student/presenter and client. For example, if the presenter is having trouble understanding or empathizing with the client, if the client is demonstrating "resistance," or the client appears disengaged with the student. Giving the client a voice in the supervision session can break through some of this (e.g., the person role-playing the client might say *I felt really shut down when you seemed not to notice I was crying*). Having another student role-play the counselor can help the presenter get in touch with emotional reactions he or she may be having to the client (e.g., *I am so frustrated that every week you haven't implemented any of the plans we discussed*). It can also help the presenter to feel empathized with (e.g., *I'm feeling anxious because this seems like an important issue and I'm not sure how to handle it*).

   b. Each group member besides the presenter takes on an area of content he or she will consider in relation to the session/client. Areas could include culture, in the moment counseling process, transference/countertransference, theoretical orientation, microskills, therapeutic alliance, values, motivation/stage of change, client emotions, client cognitions, spirituality/existential conflicts. This is a good option if the counselor/presenter is struggling in terms of the direction of the counseling, what interventions might be helpful, or counselor/client relationship issues.

The instructor can use the role assignments to build the self-efficacy of the group members who are doing the reflecting. If a student has emerged in the group as having a specific strength, such as being an advocate for clients, this is a good perspective for that student to take on and demonstrate his or her strength. Conversely, if a student struggles with cultural differences in counseling that student might benefit from stretching themselves and looking at the multicultural issues in the case.

5. With their roles/perspectives in mind the group members continue not to broadcast, but the presenter broadcasts with audio and video and presents the case, with the rest of the group as the audience. If there is a session recording to view the presenter can choose when it best fits into the presentation. The presenter concludes with asking for specific areas of feedback.

6. The presenter stops broadcasting and the other group members and the instructor then broadcast with audio and video. The presenter can see and hear everything but cannot respond verbally. The instructor should ask the presenter not to insert written chat comments while the group is reflecting.

7. The instructor invites group members to share from their perspectives/roles. If using "option a" (listed above) the instructor might say, *"Please speak as the character you were assigned about the presenters work. For example if you are speaking as the client you might say 'I felt really comforted when Sally let me cry.' These are just your hunches and intuition, you can't of course know for certain how the client felt. We are just trying to generate as much information as possible and consider new perspectives."* If using "option b" (listed above) the instructor could say, *"Please speak about what you saw or heard in terms of your content area. If you didn't see or hear anything discuss why that might be and how it might come up in the future for that client or counselor."*

8. When all the group members have had a chance to reflect and discuss, the instructor and presenter broadcast while processing the group's comments and the rest of the group stops broadcasting and observes. The instructor may begin this processing by saying, *"How did those comments sit with you?,"* or, *"In what ways was that helpful?"*

9. Time permitting, the whole group could then process the experience and allow for back and forth between the presenter and the group. See below for other process questions.

10. To wrap up the instructor should have the presenter create some specific applications or goals from what they have learned from the reflecting team process.

Discussion/Processing Questions:

Questions For Everyone in the Group After Activity is Complete:

1. What new information do you have about this case/counseling relationship/counseling encounter that you did not have before we reflected on it?
2. How was it to reflect on the work of another counselor?
3. What did you learn from the role you played or the perspective you took? About yourself? About any clients you have?

Questions for the Student Presenter:

1. What did you experience when the group was reflecting on your presentation?
2. Describe two ways you might apply what we have reflected on to work with this client or more broadly with other clients in the future.

Modifications to Activity: If the instructor is working with students prior to field experiences, any learning experience requiring the student to present his or her counseling skills could be applied to this activity. Possibilities include a review of a video or audio recording of a practice counseling session with a student/peer or a transcript of a counseling or mock counseling session.

Potential Adaptations:
If a student is visually impaired he or she could use screen modifications that are available specifically for that type of impairment. If a student is hearing impaired the activity could be conducted via written chat. Presentation materials (video, powerpoint slides, etc.) could be provided to a student ahead of time allowing the student more time to review information or modify his or her format if needed.

Cautions/Potential Issues:
Privacy of the client (or mock client) being discussed is a significant consideration. Any instructor using technology to review private information should collaborate with their institution's IT and legal departments to determine how to appropriately protect that information. Even student peers who volunteer as "mock clients" should have their privacy protected to the degree the institution decides on. Instructors should look at all materials ahead of time to ensure that disclosures by the client/peer are appropriate for class discussion and that the seriousness of the issues being discussed by the client/peer is appropriate for the skill level of the students reviewing the presentation. A password required meeting "room" helps protect client privacy, although it is important to note that many video conferencing software systems cannot guarantee privacy because software company employees and institution administrators may have access to user accounts. There are some video conference platforms that say they are HIPPAA compliant. Instructors should be aware that anything broadcast on a computer screen can be

recorded without the knowledge of the person broadcasting (Skype calls, etc.).

As with any technology, it is wise to have a plan B if technology fails-video conferences can only be successful if everyone has a good internet connection and the software is working. This author requires students to do a "test run" with their computers if they have not done a video conference using a particular platform in a while (or ever).

Credits/References:

Borders, L. D., & Brown, L. L. (2005). *The new handbook of counseling supervision.* Mahwah, NJ: Lawrence Erlbaum.

Contributing Author(s): Leah K. Clarke is an Assistant Professor of Counseling and Clinical Mental Health Track Coordinator at Messiah College. She has taught counseling in an almost exclusively online format for the past three years and is particularly interested in clinical supervision online and improving counselors' writing skills.

Chapter 22

Teaching Peer Group Supervision in an Online Environment

James Cooper-Nurse, Suzanne Mikkelson,
Elizabeth Sessoms, F.D. Boley, and Selin Philip

Goals and Learning Objectives:

1. To become a part of a peer supervision group
   a. Members will develop group cohesion through knowledge of peers, concern for peers, camaraderie, and similar activities
   b. Members will develop a group identity by being able to describe the unique personality of the group and how it relates to the personalities of members
   c. Members will take responsibility for the group by volunteering for group maintenance chores and related activities
   d. Members will learn how to establish and adhere to group norms
2. To develop the skills necessary for productive group interactions
   a. Members will learn the importance of confidentiality and how to maintain confidentiality in online environments
   b. Members will show evidence of active listening
   c. Members will display reflective listening skills, make connections, and provide helpful observations about their peers' presentations
3. To learn how to process group events
   a. Members will show an awareness of the group dynamics within their own group
   b. Members will spontaneously process group events and group dynamics
4. To learn about group dynamics in a live, experiential setting
   a. Members will show evidence of mindfulness during group meetings
   b. Members will use what they have learned experientially to inform their own work
5. To learn how to use online learning as an asset rather than an obstacle
   a. Members will utilize technology in every step of the process
   b. Members will show mastery of the technology required

c. Learning objectives will be more fully realized as members proceed through the levels of technology

Appropriate Course(s): Internship courses, specifically focusing on the Group Counseling experiences.

Point in Group When Activity is Used: This activity is intended for use throughout the Internship courses.

Estimated Time Length: This activity should require approximately 2 hours per week (1 hour preparation and 1 hour meeting) for 8 weeks.

Technology and/or Materials Needed:

1. A computer/laptop (Mac or PC) with Internet capabilities.
    ➢ Recommended Configurations:
      - Memory – 4GB or higher
      - Hard Drive – 120GB or larger
      - Sound – Speakers or integrated audio line in/out
      - Video card – Integrated or higher
      - Operating System – Mac OS X/Windows Vista (32 or 64 bit) or higher
      - Software – Internet Explorer or other web browser
      - Networking – 100/1000MB Ethernet and/or Wireless 802.11 b/g/n
      - USB 1.1 port or higher
2. Webcam with built-in microphone (compatible with Mac or PC specifications)
3. Valid school/personal email account
4. Social networking account
    ➢ LinkedIn
    ➢ Facebook
    ➢ School's online message board
5. Video chat software
    ➢ Skype
    ➢ Google+
    ➢ MSN Instant Messenger

Purpose for Suggested Technology

The purpose for the suggested hardware is to meet minimum recommended specifications for engagement in an online educational environment. Suggested software and email accounts are meant to explore movement from asynchronous communication activities (email) towards more synchronous communication activities (Facebook) including face-to-face real time chat (Skype).

Directions for Activity: This activity demonstrates the importance of peer group supervision while considering logistic and confidentiality issues in an online environment.

1. Form weekly peer groups of 4-6 students per group to discuss/consult regarding ongoing group counseling experiences.
2. Allow groups to meet for their initial peer group session via face-to-face chat. The goal for this initial session would be to establish peer group structure and schedule for members to take turns facilitating each week.
3. During the second and third weeks, groups are to communicate via email only. Facilitator responsibilities include coordination of communication, ensuring member participation, and establishing appropriate confidentiality norms.
4. During the fourth and fifth weeks, groups are to communicate via social networking means only. Facilitator responsibilities include coordination and privatization of communication, ensuring member participation, and establishing appropriate confidentiality norms.
5. During the sixth and seventh weeks, groups are to communicate via video chat software only. Facilitator responsibilities include coordination of meeting times and structuring live group format.
6. Following each format (email, social networking, video chat), students are to reflect on their experiences. These reflections are to include statements on strengths and challenges of the format as well as the importance of the peer group supervision process.

Note: Activity can be shortened or lengthened depending on the educator's desired level of student exposure to each peer group format.

Discussion/Processing Questions:

Table 1 describes an eight-week format for providing peer supervision to counseling practicum students conducting groups. To facilitate progression through the five stages of groups, suggested discussion and/or processing questions relative to the group's current stage for each week are included.

Table 1

Sample Processing Questions

WEEK	ONLINE FORMAT	GROUP PHASE	SAMPLE PROCESSING QUESTIONS
Week 1:	Face-to-Face Chat	Forming	**Sample Session Week 1** *(see Table 2)*
Week 2:	Email	Forming/Storming	How would you describe your leadership style? What type of learner are you? What goals do you hope to accomplish during peer group supervision? Reflection questions.
Week 3:	Email	Storming	What progress or challenges did you see this week in your groups? What feedback would you offer your colleague around this challenge? What techniques did you use this week to facilitate group interaction? Reflection questions
Week 4:	Social Network	Norming	What are prevalent multicultural or ethical issues that pose as potential challenges? How will you handle these issues? Are there additional suggestions within the group? Reflection questions
Week 5:	Social Network	Norming/Performing	**Sample Session Week 5** *(see Table 3)*

Week 6:	Video Chat	Performing	What case would you like to present to the group this week for processing? How have you or do you propose to handle these issues? How can we help? Reflection questions
Week 7:	Video Chat	Performing/Adjourning	What case would you like to present to the group this week for processing? How have you or do you propose to handle these issues? How can we help? Reflection questions
Week 8:	Face-to-Face Chat	Adjourning	**Sample Session Week 8** *(see Table 4)*

As referenced in Step 6 of the Activity Directions, **each session** should assess and capture the members' experience regarding each technological format. Questions guiding this process may include:

1. Today, we utilized (email, discussion board, video chat) to conduct our peer group supervisory session. How would you describe this experience?
2. What were the strengths of using this format in terms of meeting your needs? What challenges were presented?
3. Are you surprised by these findings?
4. What format do you believe has worked the best in meeting your needs? (Does not include the first session)
5. What improvements would you suggest in tweaking this format to better accomplish our goals?

In addition to the sample discussion questions referenced in Table 1are examples of how an actual one-hour peer group session could be held. These examples are referenced in Tables 2 (Week1- Forming), Table 3 (Week 5- Performing) and Table 4 (Week 8 - Adjourning). Important to note is the integration of spiritual activities (printed in italics) nested within Tables 2- 4 to provide sample options for groups conducted beyond secular settings to include religious or spiritual populations.

Table 2

Sample Session: Week 1: Forming Stage

SUGGESTED ACTIVITY	TIME SUGGESTED
**Reminder to capture group processing notes	
Greetings, Intro to Group and Goals	2 minutes
Open up in prayer – Ask for Volunteer	*2 minutes*
Spiritual Integration – Scripture.....	*2 minutes*
Questions that accomplish today's goals: • Can you each tell us your name, work, previous and present group experience? What is the type of group currently conducting?	7 minutes
• What is your greatest technological challenge with online formats? Strength?	4 minute
• What support would you need from your peers to be successful in this environment?	2 minutes
• What formats will we employ for the next seven weeks?	4 minutes
• Who will volunteer to serve as the facilitator each week?	5 minutes
• How should our cases be presented?	5 minutes
• Therefore, what should each person do to actively participate in each session?	2 minutes
• In terms of rules, how will we engage in this work? What boundaries should we set to make this an enjoyable process? What would you find as non-negotiables or must haves?	15 minutes
Review interactions of the session and closure (Closure should include reminder of the next session; time, date and format)	5 minutes
End in prayer......	5 minutes

**Religious settings may opt to use spiritual integrative techniques throughout the peer group session. Suggestions are provided in italics.

Table 3

Sample Session: Week 5: Performing Stage

SUGGESTED ACTIVITY	TIME SUGGESTED
**Reminder to capture group processing notes	
Greetings and Check in	1 minute
Open up in prayer – Ask for Volunteer	*2 minutes*
Spiritual Integration – Scripture.....	*2 minutes*
• Icebreaker: What's the last good movie you saw and what did you like about it?	5 minutes
• Case Presentation: In terms of the group sessions you've conducted since our last meeting, use the technique "Roses, Buds and Thorns" to give us a snapshot of your current experiences with your group. • Roses: something that is blooming, beautiful, and aromatic • Buds: something that you anticipate will happen or that you hope for • Thorns: something that has gotten you stuck or been difficult for you	25 minutes Each member takes turns
• Revisiting your "thorns", how do you propose to handle these unpleasant challenges?	8 minutes
• Does anyone in the group have suggestions to offer your colleague in addition to their ideas?	8 minutes
Review interactions of the session and closure (Closure should include reflection questions and reminder of the next session; time, date and format)	10 minutes
End in prayer......	5 minutes

138

**Religious settings may opt to use spiritual integrative techniques throughout the peer group session. Suggestions are provided in italics.

Table 4

Sample Session: Week 8: Adjourning Stage

SUGGESTED ACTIVITY	TIME SUGGESTED
**Reminder to capture group processing notes	
Greetings and Check in	1 minute
Open up in prayer – Ask for Volunteer	*2 minutes*
Spiritual Integration – Scripture.....	*2 minutes*
• To participate in today's session, you were asked to present an object that describes the growth/progress that you have made in this group as a leader. • Please tell us what you have brought, why you have selected this item and how it represents the growth you have made.	25 minutes
• How has this experienced\ shaped your professional identify?	8 minutes
• How will you use what you've learned and experienced in the future?	8 minutes
Review interactions of the session and closure (Closure should include reflection questions)	5 minutes
End in prayer......	5 minutes

Potential Adaptations: Group members who have disabilities such as hearing and visual impairments may require accommodations in order to fully participate in the online peer supervision experience. Though assistive technology exists to mediate access to online learning, there are several considerations that one must consider in electing to utilize technological forums to process group counseling experiences with members manifesting these disabilities. Additionally, while determining when this group member will serve as the facilitator, group members should discuss and select the appropriate technological format best suited for that member.

Deaf or Hearing Impaired

There are varying degrees of hearing impairment ranging from hard of hearing, profoundly deaf, to completely deaf (Even Grounds, 2011). Participants of all levels of hearing will be able to fully participate during weeks in which group supervision occurs via email and social networking. However, during weeks in which Skype or video-chat will be utilized, the facilitator may be required to utilize American Sign Language (ASL) (depending on the hearing level of the member). If sign language is not feasible, an interpreter should be present with the hearing impaired member to translate information and facilitate their understanding and participation within the group. When members are initially selected to participate in each group, immediately assessing the accommodations needed for deaf or hearing-impaired members enables adequate planning and inclusive means for participation by all group members.

Blind or Visually Impaired

Members who are visually impaired are capable of participating in online formats through written communications via email and other social networking programs such as LinkedIn, Facebook, and message boards. All members should be aware that visually impaired members may utilize screen readers, computerized Braille line, or text to speech programs in order to consume written information (Disabled World, 2012). However, these tools may at times delay the member's response time within the group. Additionally, charts, graphs, icons, and graphic arts should be avoided if possible. These items do not translate in the same way through assistive technology as text.

No accommodations will be required for email and social networking programs in addition to what is provided by for the blind. Screen readers, magnifiers, and reading glasses may be the extent of what is needed by the group member in order to participate. They may already employ enlarged font, plain text, and the like while using JAWS or other text to speech programs (Disabled World, 2012). Written communications to include agendas or activities that will be presented during the supervision session and read by participants should be submitted prior to the session. This will allow the member to utilize any assistive technology needed to read and gather information in preparation for the group.

Cautions/Potential Issues: Cautions or potential issues to consider when implementing the weekly peer group activities, including possible technology issues that may not be common knowledge are provided below.

Recommendations for handling potential barriers have also been included as suggested resolutions.

1. Develop and email a schedule to all members that includes the meeting time, facilitator, and mode of meeting for each week
2. Send weekly notifications to peer group members to remind them of the meeting format.
3. Establish methods for reaching out to members who are absent from a given meeting
4. Assign a scribe for the week to capture the essential elements of the group discussion
5. While establishing group norms, discuss consequences when members fail to attend several group meetings without prior notification
6. During the initial session, establish online etiquette including session slang, shorthand, tone, capitalization, exclamation marks, etc...
7. Peer group members' skill levels may vary in effectively utilizing various methods of technology therefore members should be advised to seek training to bolster competency in any technological format in which they are weak
8. To minimize impacts on technological glitches, methods for rectifying or providing technical assistance in a timely fashion should be suggested
9. Identify an alternative technological method for group member's participation if access to the identified format is impeded
10. Members should be advised to download all software and establish social networking accounts prior to the designated date of class
11. All programs and accounts should be tested to ensure all glitches are addressed removing potential barriers to group participation

These recommendations are suggested as a result of common impediments to peer group supervision previously experienced by the authors. Utilizing these suggestions will enable all members to plan for success while overcoming obstacles to learning

Credits/References:

Disabled World. (2012, April 11). [Website]. Retrieved from http://www.disabled-world.com/assistivedevices/computer/screen-readers.php

Even Grounds, Inc. (2011). [Website]. Retrieved from http://www.evengrounds.com/articles/how-do-people-with-different-disabilities-use-the-computer

Contributing Author(s): James Cooper-Nurse is a doctoral student in the Counselor Education and Supervision program at Regent University. His areas of interest include counselor development, multicultural issues in counseling and supervision, counseling theory, childhood trauma, and the use of technology in counseling.

Suzanne Mikkelson is a doctoral student in the Counselor Education and Supervision program at Regent University. Her areas of interest include Marriage and Family Therapy (particularly parenting issues and adultery recovery), emotion-focused couple therapy, eye movement desensitization reprocessing for trauma recovery, spiritual integration in counseling, and counselor supervision.

Elizabeth Sessoms is a doctoral student in the Counselor Education and Supervision program at Regent University. Her areas of interest include school counselor development and supervision, college and career readiness (assessment and planning), reconciliation and conflict resolution, addictions counseling, child sexual abuse and trauma, and CISM and grief counseling.

F. D. Boley is a doctoral student in the Counselor Education and Supervision program at Regent University. His areas of interest include philosophical anthropology, the integration of philosophy and theology with psychology, character education, virtue ethics, and cognitive science and psychotherapies.

Selin Philip is a doctoral student in the Counselor Education and Supervision program at Regent University. Her areas of interest include trauma and resilience, the development of university students (special focus on international students), integration of spirituality and holistic approaches in counseling, couples/family counseling, women's issues, grief counseling, and culture and diversity.

ACITIVITES for ASSESSMENT and RESEARCH METHODS

Chapter 23

The 60/40 Split

Leann M. Wyrick-Morgan, Kevin P. Gosselin, and Brianna Moore

Goals and Learning Objectives:
1. Enhance learning of course materials by challenging students to provide evidentiary support for answers and build group interaction through guided collaborative learning
2. To create meaningful arguments, supported by evidence for why answers are correct
3. To present work to a classroom group much like colleagues in the field, thus simulating a professional environment within the coursework
4. To select, conduct, and report appropriate statistics to test hypotheses as demonstrated by ability to present agreed upon concepts to the group
5. Identify and test assumptions for statistical tests as evidenced by ability to present and support reasoning to the group
6. Appropriately interpret reported statistical findings, as evidenced by ability to present interpretation to the group and gain support for answers

Assessment of Learning Objectives: Measurement of the above learning outcomes include, individual course exam scores that will be used to assess students' knowledge surrounding the material. Secondly, students' ability to articulate and convey a working knowledge of the course content will be measured by the group scores on the exams.

Appropriate Course(s): Research Methods, and/or Tests and Measurement

When in Group Activity is Used: The authors encourage using this exercise early in the semester, prior to the first "drop/add date," so students may assess their own performance and determine if they are adequately prepared for the workload in the course. Although the activity can be structured for implementation at various times over the duration of a course, it is recommended to implement this early in the semester to establish group cohesiveness within online courses.

Estimated Time Length: This exercise is broken down into 3 units (one every 5 weeks). It is completed over a 6-day period, including 4 days for individual work and 2 days for group review. The frequency in which this activity is adopted can be adjusted to accommodate differing course content, assessment structure, and instructional styles.

Technology and/or Materials Needed:
Explanation Using Less Technology:

Students may use traditional email methods to circulate a Word document that contains each group member's ideas. One member creates the document with her/his answers and then forwards the document to others in the group. Each group member chooses a distinct color and codes her/his answers/input in that color only. The members send the document to all group members as it is "discussed" until all members agree to the final draft of the answers. Another way to complete this exercise is through the use of "Google Docs" or "Drop Box" where the document can be circulated or accessed by all group members simultaneously, without waiting for it to progress around the group members' email accounts. Ideally, if students have access to "Blackboard" or "Moodle," students could post their answers to their Discussion Board and "discuss" why each is valid, while deciding which answer represents the "voice" of the group.

Explanation Using Additional Technology:

Another option is the use of programs like "Eluminate" where students can live chat via webcam with one another, while collaboratively viewing a "working document" that each member can contribute to seamlessly. This type of technology requires additional software be made available to students, and each student would have to have access to a webcam with a microphone. It does take some getting used to, but students typically enjoy the freedom of being able to collaboratively work on documents in real time. This process also cuts down on time, because they can log on and work together, as opposed to waiting for a document to be emailed among the group several times. When group members have the ability to interact and see one another, another potential advantage associated with conducting the activity through live interactive web sessions is that students may establish a greater rapport with each other through communication methods that better emulate face to face interactions.

Directions for Activity:

1. The instructor provides students with one course exam or learning unit.
2. Students complete the exam or unit on their own and return to instructor after 4 days.
3. The instructor randomly assigns students to "working groups."
4. The students then are allowed to contact the members of their group to discuss the exam and create a set of answers as agreed upon by the group.

5. After 48 hours, the groups submit their answers to the instructor.
6. The instructor then grades the individual exams and the group exams (or units) and provides students with results.
7. The grades are then weighted at: 60% for the individual grade and 40% for the group grade totaling 100% of the possible points earned for that exam or unit.

Discussion/Processing Questions:

1. What did you learn from your classmates about the material that you didn't know or were unsure about before the collaboration?
2. How did you contribute to the group collaborative process? In what ways?
3. What did you find most helpful as a result of this process?
4. What did you find most distressing as a result of this process?

Potential Adaptations: Some adaptations that could make the activity more user friendly for those with challenges could be to allow more time for individuals to work on the group document (72 hours), or perhaps circulating a Word document in extra-large print. In addition, the instructor could conduct oral discussions via Elluminate (or Skype) for group process, and instructors should provide assistance needed to accommodate specific needs of students within the group.

Cautions/Potential Issues:

1. Students competing with one another as opposed to collaborating on the exam.
2. The nature of the course (statistics/research) may heighten performance anxiety of group members' feelings of inadequacy and self-efficacy beliefs to be successful in the course.
3. Students may experience difficulty in reconciling differences regarding "correct" exam/unit answers.
4. Some students may "give in" and allow the group to present an incorrect answer rather than disrupt the group process and be viewed as "difficult."

Credits/References: Credit for this exercise goes to Dr. Kevin Gosselin from The University of Texas at Tyler who created this group exercise for use in his online "Advanced Statistical Methods" course.

Contributing Author(s): Dr. Leann M. Wyrick-Morgan is an Assistant Professor of Counseling in the Department of Counseling and Human Services at The University of Colorado, Colorado Springs.

Dr. Kevin P. Gosselin is an Assistant Professor of Biostatistics in the College of Nursing and Health Sciences at The University of Texas at Tyler.

Brianna Moore is a doctoral student in Epidemiology at Colorado State University.

Chapter 24

Clearer Research through Messy Thinking: Developing a Counseling Research Project

Lauren Paulson and Jodi Sindlinger

Goals and Learning Objectives: The following student learning outcomes are in compliance with ACA and CACREP standards:

1. Assist group members in identifying, defining, and understanding basic research methodologies, theories, and analyses applicable to the field of counseling
2. To understand the importance and challenges of conducting research in the counseling field through a self-designed research study
3. To describe and apply ethical and legal issues relevant to counseling research.
4. Assist group members to connect and explain the interrelationship between research, practice, and program development by engaging in meaningful dialogue with other students and the instructor

Appropriate Course(s): Research Methods course and Counseling Thesis class.

Point in Group When Activity is Used: This activity can be implemented at the beginning of the semester in a Research Methods course, or a Counseling Thesis class where students develop a proposal or implement a research project.

Estimated Time Length: This session requires at least one class session, however, the activity can be adapted over several class sessions.

Technology and/or Materials Needed: This activity requires asynchronous (email, drop box) and synchronous electronic communication technologies.

<u>Minimum Requirements:</u>

1. Computer with speakers, an attached headset, and video camera are highly recommended. Students' sense of isolation can be alleviated with the incorporation of video technology (Panos, 2005).
2. Online course management system. Examples include Blackboard, Moodle, and Desire2Learn.
3. Internet access: Broadband access (DSL, cable) is highly recommended, but not mandatory.

Most available online course management systems include the instruction, discussion, and interaction tools required for this activity. Group break out rooms, audio, video, electronic whiteboard, and application sharing are the minimum requirements to deliver the activity as described.

Computer Requirements:

The quality of technology available to implement on-line activities may affect student experiences. Below are the specific recommended technological requirements for this activity if you are using Blackboard's Course Management System.

Participant Requirements:

- Windows 2000+, Mac OSX 10.3+* or Linux**
- 128 MB RAM (256 MB recommended)
- IE 6.0+, Safari 1.2+, Firefox 1.5 - 2.0 (Browser must be Java and JavaScript enabled)
- Internet access at 56k or above

Instructor Requirements:

- Windows 2000+, Mac OSX 10.3+* or Linux**
- 256 MB RAM (higher recommended)
- IE 6.0+, Safari 1.2+, Firefox 1.5 - 2.0 (Browser must be Java and JavaScript enabled)
- Internet access at 56k or above (Broadband strongly recommended)

* Mac OS X 10.3 is not supported for Wimba Classroom 5.1.1+
* IE for Mac not supported
** Presenters cannot display content via Application Sharing using Linux. However, participants using Linux can view.
**Audio and video is only compatible with Linux on Wimba Classroom versions 4.2+
Broadband Internet connection or higher recommended

Recommended Course Management System:

Most course management systems including, Blackboard, Moodle, and Desire2Learn, allow multifunctional applications. Specifically, Blackboard's Wimba Classroom 6.1 supports online interaction (Breakout Rooms) and presentation (eBoard Tools). The Wimba Classroom eBoard Tools allow participants to draw shapes and lines, type text, and import graphics to create interaction when working on group assignments. Students may upload graphics or PowerPoint slides before the class session and/or use the eBoard tools live during the class session. Breakout Rooms allow students to meet in small groups within the online classroom. Instructors can send

public and private messages to all participants within a Breakout Room and bring content from the breakout rooms into the main classroom. Wimba stores all content that students upload, including a Chat Log record, so the instructor can view, save, or print all online events. Student and instructor guides are available at
http://www.wimba.com/services/support/documentation#wCl

Directions for Activity:

Introduction:

This activity, adapted from Nelson and Paisley (2001), is useful in a class where students are given opportunities to collaborate or give/get feedback related to a research proposal or project. The online class discussions provide the opportunity for an in-depth, rich, and reflective learning experience. In most cases, the instructor should facilitate group processing through Socratic questioning and provide guided prompts to promote higher-order thinking, problem-solving, and deeper understanding. The instructor may use a number of online tools to do this—for example, "dropping in" during small group work, "whispering" input to students, posing questions, and/ or considerations to the whole group using the whiteboard. This interaction allows for problem solving, social negotiation, expanding and explaining knowledge, and critical thinking surrounding topics of research (Driscoll, 2000; Millis, 2002; Nelson & Neufeldt, 1998). Specific prompts the instructor can use include: Can you say that another way? What is another way to look at it? What assumptions have you made? What should you do with this new information? Instructors can program the record setting (or Archive setting in Wimba) to capture all actions that occurred including: audio and video, public text comments, and application sharing that can be posted or downloaded as MP4 video or MP3 audio.

Pre-activity:

1. With a general research topic area of interest in mind, students prepare for the activity by individually developing a "Thought Mess" (Nelson & Paisley, 2001). A thought mess is "a visual depiction, a diagram or graph, that represents a student's current conceptual thinking in a particular subject area" (Nelson & Paisley, 2001, p. 129). The student should think about their topical area related to the field of counseling and where there are gaps in knowledge. This allows students a voice in selecting and shaping their own research topic of interest. Students are encouraged to "think big" and consider multiple perspectives or ways at looking at the problem. The instructor can share an example of a thought mess to provide structure and scaffolding (See below).

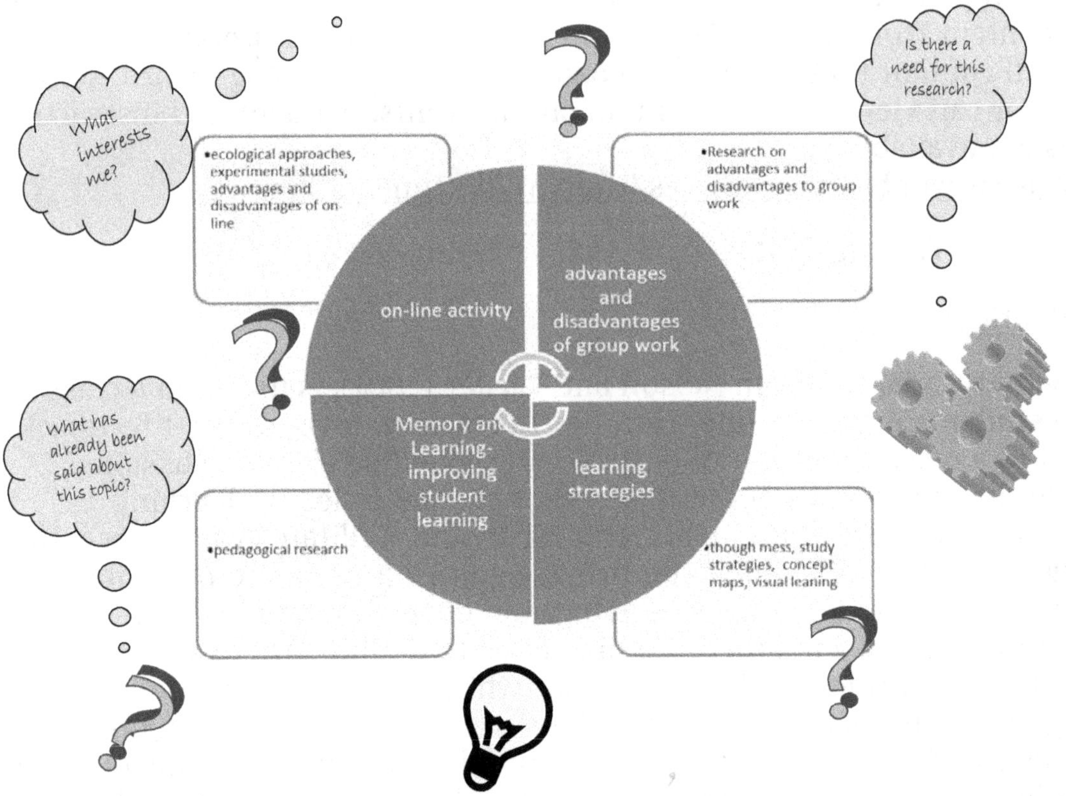
What interests me?
Is there a need for this research?
What has already been said about this topic?
•ecological approaches, experimental studies, advantages and disadvantages of on-line
•Research on advantages and disadvantages to group work
on-line activity
advantages and disadvantages of group work
Memory and Learning- improving student learning
learning strategies
•pedagogical research
•though mess, study strategies, concept maps, visual leaning

2. Prior to the online session, students will submit their diagram to the instructor's drop box.

<u>Online Activity</u>:

1. In breakout rooms, groups of 3 students will present their thought mess documents (uploaded to eBoard) to other group members.

2. Using various online tools such as multi-way audio, follow the speaker video, public chat, and emoticons, group members provide feedback, raise questions, and help the student restructure and clarify their ideas. For example, mutli-way audio allows students to talk and be heard, follow the speaker video automatically switches recording via voice activation, and emoticons facilitate social connectivity. This visual and creative process is multidimensional and requires students to access knowledge, skills, and attitudes. This interaction allows students to test and challenge constructed reality and one-dimensional thinking through social interaction and negotiation (Driscoll, 2000; Lambert & McCombs, 1998). The idea is for students to "struggle" with their ideas in a creative manner (Nelson & Pailsey, 2001, p.129), using technology and their group members to aid in the process.

3. Question's students could consider include: Based on the counseling literature, what is known about the topic? What is missing? What needs to be known? Students will not need to write down or formally answer the above processing questions as the software program will record their voices and archive their typed comments for later reference.

4. The instructor can monitor the groups' ability to stay on task and mitigate conflict by sending public and private messages. Additionally, PowerPoint slides may be uploaded in the Breakout rooms, as needed.

<u>Post Class Activity</u>:
1. Students will begin to shape their research topic and develop preliminary research questions to be submitted to the instructor through the drop box.
2. Finally, students will complete a reflection log of the experience and submit online for credit prior to leaving the online classroom.

Discussion/Processing Questions:
1. What is your research area of interest? Why are you interested in this topic?
2. What is known on the topic? What is missing? What needs to be known?
3. What was the messiest or muddiest point for you in this process?
4. What have you learned about the process of constructing counseling research? Did you discover any new insights? What questions do you still have?
5. What contributions did you make in your breakout group (submitted assignments on time, participated in discussions, etc.)?

Potential Adaptations: Instructors can take advantage of the online environment and invite collaboration with other disciplines or "experts" in the field to process the activity. For example, the instructor could invite a qualitative researcher to the class to provide alterative perspectives. In addition, the instructor can have the students "meet" as a large group in the online classroom to process the small group activity.

Most course management systems provide several adaptations for persons with disabilities. Specifically using Wibma, for those who are blind or have low vision, adaptations include scalable content, personalized color/contrast schemes, slide descriptions, and full reader support. A door chime and hand raised chime, notifying presenters when an individual enters/exits Wimba Classroom or has raised their hand, can be enabled by default within this interface. For those who are hard of hearing or deaf the following adaptations can be implemented closed captioning, text messaging, a text timeline documenting activities during the session, voice recognition input, and session archiving. Finally for students with learning disabilities, breakout rooms for one-on-one mentoring and one-to-one video is an option to address individual learning needs.

Cautions/Potential Issues: As with all technology, there is a potential for failure and technical malfunction. Many online classroom management systems allow for Telephone Simulcast as a backup option for users allowing participants to listen and talk via standard phone line. In addition to an online presence, instructors should be available to students via phone and e-mail for additional support. Instructors should also assess their students' familiarity and comfort level with using the technology suggested in this and other online activities to minimize student frustration and/or miscommunication (Sindlinger, 2011).

Credits/References:

Driscoll, M. P. (2000). *Psychology of learning for instruction* (2ⁿᵈ ed.). Needham Heights, MA: Allyn & Bacon.

Millis, B. J. (2002). Enhancing learning-and more!- through cooperative learning. *IDEA paper No. 38.* Manhattan, KS: Kansas State University, Center for Faculty Evaluation and Development.

Nelson, M. L. & Neufeldt, S. A. (1998). The pedagogy of counseling: A critical examination [Electronic version]. *Counselor Education and Supervision, 38,* 70-88.

Nelson, M. L. & Paisley, P. O. (2001). Teaching counseling research from a constructivist perspective. In Eriksen, K. & McAuliffe, G. (Eds.). (2001). *Teaching counselors and therapists: Constructivist and developmental course design.* Westport, Connecticut: Bergin & Garvey.

Panos, P. T. (2005). A model for using videoconferencing technology to support international social work field practicum students. *International Social Work, 48,* 834-841.

Sindlinger, J. (2011). *Doctoral students experience with using the reflecting team model of supervision online.* Duquesne University). *ProQuest Dissertations and Theses,* http://search.proquest.com/docview/885366427?accountid=13901

Contributing Author(s): Dr. Lauren Paulson earned her doctorate in Counselor Education and Supervision from Duquesne University and currently is a Assistant Professor at Allegheny College. She has 13 years of experience in clinical work providing both individual and group counseling, and 4 years of experience teaching at both the undergraduate and graduate level, including group counseling. Her scholarly interests include issues related to rural mental health, counselor education and supervision, and eating disorders.

Dr. Jodi Sindlinger earned her doctorate in Counselor Education and Supervision from Duquesne University. She is an experienced group counselor and instructor of group counseling techniques. Her scholarly interests include using innovative approaches in teacher and counselor preparation and supervising clinical experiences for school counselors.

Chapter 25
Engaging Online Students: Incorporating Group Techniques with Technology

Pamela H. Sickinger and Mark D. Newmeyer

Goals and Learning Objectives:
1. Students will be active participants in the online classroom
   Objective 1: Using online polling for open ended responses, all students will complete a low-stakes writing assignment simulating the Go Around technique
   Objective 2: Using the discussion board forum, students will create a post addressing the processing questions and follow up with responses to classmates' posts
2. Students will increase interactions with classmates
   Objective 1: Using break-out rooms, all students will participate in small group case conference style discussions
   Objective 2: Using modified group counseling techniques, the instructor will facilitate student participation in the classroom and on the discussion board
3. Students will apply what they have learned in the course to an authentic problem
   Objective 1: Each group will: a) develop an assessment battery; b) make a brief presentation to the class summarizing recommendations; and c) respond to questions regarding their work
4. The instructor will increase interactions with students
   Objective 1: Taking on the role of supervisor, the instructor will offer feedback on each group's case conference discussion
   Objective 2: The instructor will facilitate a follow-up discussion board exercise to process the experience with students

Appropriate Course(s): This activity is intended for use in an Assessment class, but can be easily adapted to any core counselor education course that utilizes the case study as a learning tool.

Point in Group When Activity is Used: Polling and breakout rooms can be used at any point in the class; however, this activity is most suitable for the middle to end of this course. Before students can accurately propose the use of specific instruments, they need to have working knowledge of a range of assessment options as well as the typical components of a full assessment battery. They also need to have a level of trust built up with peers to be comfortable engaging in discussion.

Estimated Time Length: The total length of this activity depends on the number of groups in the class. Assuming four group presentations, it can be covered in 90 minutes. The follow up discussion board can be time limited by the instructor to one week or less.

- Case review – 5-10 minutes
- Small group case conference discussions – 30 minutes
- Class presentations – 10 minutes per group
- Low stakes writing – 5 minutes
- Discussion Board – asynchronous; can be carried out over several days to conclude on a date established by the instructor

Technology and/or Materials Needed:

- Online course software, e.g. Blackboard 9.1
- Synchronous classroom, e.g. Wimba Classroom 6.1

To use Wimba Classroom 6.1, you will need the following:

- Windows 7, Vista or XP; Mac OSX 10.4+
- 256 MB RAM
- Internet Explorer 7.0+, Safari 3.0+, Firefox 3.0+ (Java and Javascript enabled)
- Internet access at 56K or above

(http://www.wimba.com/products/wimba_classroom/Vendor)

- Webcam
- Microphone and speakers or combination headset

Purpose of Technology

Wimba Classroom 6.1 is a virtual classroom that is connected with Blackboard 9.1 (the platform in which the online education program is conducted).

Directions for Activity:

1. Prior to the online class meeting, the instructor will create a synchronous classroom, including an open ended poll to use as a version of the *Go Around* technique. The question to be posed is, *"What was this group exercise like for you?"* Next, the instructor will establish breakout rooms to be used for group discussion. There should be a sufficient number to accommodate dividing the class into groups of four. The instructor should pre-determine how groups will be organized (voluntary, assignment by specific criteria, alphabetical, etc.) Finally, the instructor should set up a discussion board forum, to be opened to students immediately following the class meeting.

2. As the class opens, the instructor details the goals for the session. Instructions for the activity are shared. Questions are answered and group assignments are made.

3. Details of a fictitious case study (based on information that would be collected during an intake/diagnostic interview) are posted on the whiteboard. This case should be somewhat complex, including elements such as diversity, ethics, social justice issues, etc. The instructor, acting in the role of supervisor, discusses the case and then provides a brief review of the major categories of instruments used in an assessment battery. Students are then given the charge to spend 30 minutes, in their groups, consulting with each other to develop recommendations of specific instruments to include in the assessment battery and to provide a rationale for their choices. They are also told that they will need to make a brief presentation of their recommendations to the class.

4. While groups are meeting, the instructor enters each breakout room and, still acting in the role of supervisor, provides feedback and/or poses questions to stimulate discussion with students. At the end of the 30 minute time frame, groups return to the classroom.

5. Each group is given 10 minutes to present their recommendations for the assessment battery. Together with the instructor, other students are invited to comment and ask questions of the presenting group.

6. At the conclusion of the presentations, the instructor tells students that they are going to complete a five minute writing exercise to discuss their group's work. The open ended poll question is displayed and students are directed to type their responses.

7. When five minutes have elapsed, the instructor asks students to submit their work. Once all responses have been received, the instructor reviews and publishes them for the class. Students then have the opportunity to see what others wrote and can make connections between their experiences.

8. The instructor tells students that an asynchronous discussion board will be opened with an initial post to help them process their group experience (see section 8 for detail). Students are told that they must post their own responses and then, through follow up postings, actively engage in discussion with the instructor and other group members.

Discussion/Processing Questions: This is an example of how the instructor may facilitate processing the group exercise through the use of the discussion board forum. It is based on Stockton, Morran, and Nitza's (2000) *cognitive map*. As students post, the instructor can comment and question students about their group experiences. This serves as both a form of feedback and a method of promoting student interaction.

Sample Post to Discussion Board

Reflecting on your small group experience, identify a significant event that occurred during your group's attempt to come to consensus on the assessment battery exercise. This can be a conflict, a suggestion that elicited a strong reaction (positive or negative), or any event that you felt was pivotal to group member interactions.

1. Describe the significant event. What happened? Why does this event stand out for you as being significant?
2. Discuss how you thought and felt about it. What impact did it have on you?
3. As a result of this event, what did you learn about yourself, the other group members, and/or the group as a whole?

Please post your response within 24 hours. To promote discussion, please respond to classmates' posts and instructor comments.

Potential Adaptations:

Visual Impairments

Technology used by those with visual impairments to access online education includes screen readers and screen magnifiers (Crow, 2008). For example, Blackboard 9.1 provides tutorials that demonstrate use of the JAWS screen reader to complete a variety of tasks in that format (Blackboard, 2012). Wimba Classroom 6.1 also provides support for use of the JAWS screen reader (Wimba, 2010). In addition, instructors can design their course layout to be more user friendly. For those with visual impairments, accessibility can be enhanced through use of alt tags to identify elements that a screen reader cannot read such as pictures and tables (Crow, 2008).

Hearing Impairments

In the Wimba Classroom 6.1 format, there are two options for making live presentations accessible to the student with a hearing impairment – closed captioning and TDD services (Wimba, 2010). With closed captioning, the captioner is present in the class so as to provide real time text of the session proceedings. The TDD option is available for students who wish to use Wimba's phone-in access with a relay operator (Wimba, 2010).

Learning Disabilities

Students with learning disabilities should follow university protocol for requesting accommodations. Instructors can make their courses more accessible for these individuals by keeping them visually well-organized and uncluttered (Crow, 2008). In this sample activity, students with memory or attention issues may benefit from having a hard copy of the case study to use for reference. Additionally, these individuals can access the Wimba Classroom archive to help with recall of details from the discussions.

Cautions/Potential Issues: Access to Wimba Classroom 6.1 is available through the Internet and by phone. The phone alternative is especially helpful when a student experiences computer connectivity issues. Beyond this basic technological consideration, the following recommendations may be useful:
1. The instructor should be fully conversant in the use of online polling and breakout rooms. Technical manuals and tutorials are available to assist with implementing these features.
2. The instructor must monitor time spent with students in each of the breakout rooms to allow for equitable contact with all groups.

Credits/References:

Blackboard. (2012). *Additional accessibility information and resources.* Retrieved from http://www.blackboard.com/Platforms/Learn/Resources/Accessibility/JAWS-Demo.aspx

Crow, K. L. (2008). Four types of disabilities: Their impact on online learning. *Tech Trends,* 5 2(1), 51-55.

Stockton, R., Morran, D. K. & Nitza, A. G. (2000). Processing group events: A conceptual map for leaders. *The Journal for Specialists in Group Work,* 25, 343-355. doi: 10.1080/01933920008411678

Wimba. (2010). *Wimba classroom accessibility best practices guide.* Retrieved from http://www.wimba.com/assets/resources/WC_Accessibility.pdf

Contributing Author(s): Pamela H. Sickinger, M.Ed., is a doctoral candidate in the Counselor Education and Supervision program at Regent University. She is currently interning in a private practice that specializes in clients with Autism Spectrum Disorder diagnoses, conducting groups that focus on social skills, communication, and transition issues. A certified school counselor for over twenty years, she is interested in adolescent issues, specifically, career development and the transition to post-high school life. She enjoys reading, solving crossword puzzles, indulging her creative interests, and spending time with her husband and children.

Mark D. Newmeyer, Ed.D. is an Assistant Professor in the School of Psychology and Counseling at Regent University. He is a licensed professional clinical counselor in Ohio and Virginia. Dr. Newmeyer is a professional member of the American Counseling Association, which recognized his achievements by honoring him in 2004 as an Emerging Leader. He also serves as co-chair of Training Standards Committee for the Association of Specialists in Group Work (ASGW). When not involved with his work Mark enjoys running, reading, and spending time with his family and friends.

Chapter 26

Putting the Pieces Together: Using Online Groups to Teach Principles of Comprehensive Client Assessment

Jodi Sindlinger and Lauren Paulson

Goals and Learning Objectives: The expected outcome of this activity is in line with CACREP Standards (2009) relating to knowledge and skills required for assessment and evaluation in a multicultural society.
1. Explore the concept of assessment as a *process* of collecting and integrating data from multiple methods and multiple sources.
2. Be able to explain the importance of a comprehensive approach to accurate client assessment and appraisal.

Appropriate Course(s): This activity could be used in an introductory course or a course specific to training counselors in assessment and evaluation. The activity of putting together pieces of a puzzle replicates a comprehensive approach to counseling in that the activity involves students in the process of collecting data from numerous sources and engaging multiple perspectives of client issues. By adapting the content of the case study, this activity could be used to meet additional CACREP standards in social and cultural diversity, career development, research, and group work.

Point in Group When Activity is Used: This activity could be used to introduce course concepts and/or to illustrate more complex concepts and applications with modification.

Estimated Time Length: This activity, as described, could be completed in one class session. With modification, the activity could easily be extended, revisited, and/or further processed throughout the semester.

Technology and/or Materials Needed:

Minimum Requirements:
1. Computer with speakers, and attached headset, and video camera are highly recommended. Students' sense of isolation can be alleviated with the incorporation of video technology (Panos, 2005).
2. Internet access: Broadband access (DSL, cable) is highly recommended.

3. Online course management system.

The interaction (Breakout Rooms) and presentation (eBoard Tools) methods described here are features of *Wimba Classroom 6.1*, although most available online course management student systems include the instruction, discussion, and interaction tools required for this activity. Group break out rooms, audio, video, electronic whiteboard, and application sharing features are recommended to deliver the activity as described. The quality of technology available to implement on-line activities may affect student experiences. Below are recommended requirements for using Wimba for this activity. Additional considerations for using Wimba are available at http://www.wimba.com/services/support/documentation#wCl

Participant Requirements

- Windows 2000+, Mac OSX 10.3+* or Linux**
- 128 MB RAM (256 MB recommended)
- IE 6.0+, Safari 1.2+, Firefox 1.5 - 2.0 (Browser must be Java and JavaScript enabled)
- Internet access at 56k or above

Instructor Requirements

- Windows 2000+, Mac OSX 10.3+* or Linux**
- 256 MB RAM (higher recommended)
- IE 6.0+, Safari 1.2+, Firefox 1.5 - 2.0 (Browser must be Java and JavaScript enabled)
- Internet access at 56k or above (Broadband strongly recommended)

Directions for Activity: The directions for this activity include five steps, (1) preparation, (2):a piece of the puzzle, (3) working the puzzle, (4) processing and reflection.

Step 1: Preparation

1. Set up online classroom, provide students with training and practice in navigating online classroom features.

2. Develop and assign reading materials (for example, a case study) and upload to online classroom content.

3. Divide students into small groups of 3-5 students.

4. Assign time to meet in online classroom and provide brief instructions for students to view upon signing in to the class session.

In this activity, small groups of students will explore isolated issues of assessment and later combine their findings into a comprehensive picture of a client. In this example, the instructor divided a class of 12 students into three small groups of 4. The instructor provided each group with a partial case study appearing in a course textbook. The case study selected included a description of the client, and data from a parent interview including developmental history, family background, interview data, teacher's observational reports, results from intelligence testing and from a home behavior parent checklist. Instructors should identify or develop a case study prior to onset of this activity. When teaching students with a child and adolescent focus, the instructor may find Wilmshurst's casebook helpful (2011). Other collections of case studies for specific interests (child and adolescent, psychoeducational, adult, career-oriented) are available through the American Psychological Association (www.APA.org) and Pearson Publishing (www.pearsonhighered.com). The instructor pre-assigned topics to each group of students related to their portion of the case study. In this example, group 1 was assigned "background information," group 2, behavioral observations, and group 3, test results. Any number of interrelated aspects of assessment can be used for this activity. Other examples of 3 inter related assessment topics that could be used to promote understanding might include: Issues of Reliability, Validity, and Usability; Interviews, Observations, Test Scores; Educational, Vocational, and Social factors; and Ethics, Cultural, and Developmental Considerations, etc.

In cases where students have had limited exposure to online interaction and/or instruction, instructors should considering using test runs to make certain that students have practiced accessing the online classroom and participating in the activity. The instructor should plan to be available to students via phone and e-mail for additional support, and to advise students on accessing technical assistance during the activity. An early assessment of students' familiarity and comfort level with using the technology suggested in this and other online activities is recommended so that student frustration and/or miscommunication is minimized(Sindlinger, 2011).

Step 2:   A Piece of the Puzzle (Small Group Work)

Upon signing in to the class session, students receive group assignments and instructions to go to online break out rooms. In each break out room, students access the assigned portion of the case study and begin to discussion around the assigned topic. The assigned portion of the case study is considered a "piece" of the puzzle depicting the client. In this portion of the activity, students should be encouraged to collaborate and/or get feedback related to their understanding of the client's presentation.

During the small, online group discussions the instructor should facilitate an in-depth, rich, and reflective learning experience. Socratic questioning and other prompts (Griffith & Frieden, 2000) aimed at promoting higher-order thinking and inquiry-based learning should be delivered through the online classroom functions. In online classrooms, these typically include "dropping in" on each student group, "whispering," and/or delivering written prompts using an e-board function. The instructor should pose questions to the group to guide them to verbalize and/or illustrate using online tools, what they know about the client based on the information given, and also to discover what additional information they need to know to have an informed picture of the client. Questions the instructor might pose include "what is the issue? "What do you believe is true about this client," "What information about this client would contradict your current impression?" "What would you like to know about this client that you do not already know?"

The instructor might also use this time to facilitate processing, clarify misunderstandings, promote multiple perspectives, and/or pose questions or additional considerations to individuals or small groups. The intention of this part of the activity is to engage students in problem solving, social negotiation, expanding and explaining knowledge, and critical thinking surrounding topics relating to assessment (Nelson & Neufeldt, 1998). Instructors can program the sessions to capture audio and video, public text comments, and application sharing that can be posted in the online classroom or downloaded as MP4 video or MP3 audio for later reference or further processing.

Students should use similar online tools (such as multi-way audio, follow the speaker video, public chat, emoticons, and other eBoard tools) to provide feedback, raise questions, share, and clarify their assessment of the client according to the portion of the case study they were assigned. They should end by posting 5-10 specific questions they have about the client using the online classroom tools. The students should be able to upload other course material, including power point slides and articles of reference within the small group and share with the larger group as they complete the "puzzle."

Step3:Working the Puzzle (Large Group Work)

The instructor invites all students to return to the main classroom. Each group takes turns to present their understanding of the client and their list of unanswered questions.

Step4:Discussion and Processing

(See Below – Discussion/Processing Questions)

Discussion/Processing Questions: For the first part of step 4 (Discussion and Processing), the instructor encourages students in the large group, students to share their reactions to the information provided by other groups. The instructor should facilitate reflection by posting questions to the e-board or within the text window. Questions appropriate for this stage of the activity may include the following:

1. How does the information from other groups "fit" with your piece of the puzzle?
2. What are you finding out now that you did not expect to hear?
3. What are you hearing that confirms your impressions of this client?
4. What questions remain unanswered for you at this point?

This part concludes when students suggest solutions or "complete the puzzle" based on their synthesis of puzzle pieces into a completed picture (accurate assessment). In the second part of step 4, the instructor should pose questions to facilitate learning including:

1. What insight do you have about the assessment process in light of this activity?
2. What was it like to only have part of the puzzle?
3. What is the counselor's role in putting together a client's puzzle (accurately assessing a client)? What is the client's role?
4. How much does our completed puzzle look like the picture on the box?
5. What if someone looses a piece of this puzzle or makes it fit in where it does not belong?

Instructors have the option of following this activity with an additional assignment that might include asking students to submit a written journal entry, participate in a reflective online discussion, and/or develop a written assessment report based on this case study..

Potential Adaptations: Wimba 6.1 provides several adaptations for persons with disabilities. For example, for those who are blind or have low vision adaptations include scalable content, personalized color/contrast schemes, slide descriptions, and full reader support. A door chime and hand raised chime, notifying presenters when an individual enters/exits Wimba Classroom or has raised their hand, can be enabled by default. For those who are hard of hearing or deaf the following adaptations can be implemented: closed captioning, text messaging, a text timeline documenting activities during the session, voice recognition input, and session archiving. Finally, providing written materials in advance, and additional one-on-one online mentoring and discussion are options to address individual learning needs.

Cautions/Potential Issues: As with all technology, there is a potential for failure and technical malfunction. Many online classroom management systems allow for telephone participation as a backup option for users allowing participants to listen and talk via standard phone line. Students should be able to access the online classroom's help feature, technical guides, and troubleshooting menus. Instructors should also assess their students' familiarity and comfort level with using the technology suggested in this and other online activities to minimize student frustration and/or miscommunication (Sindlinger, 2011). Instructors should be available to students via phone and e-mail for additional support prior to and following this activity.

Credits/References:

Griffith, B. & Frieden, G. (2000). Facilitating reflective thinking. *Counselor Education & Supervision, 40(2)*, 82-92.

Nelson, M. L. & Neufeldt, S. A. (1998). The pedagogy of counseling: A critical examination [Electronic version]. *Counselor Education and Supervision,* 38, 70-88.

Panos, P. T. (2005). A model for using videoconferencing technology to support international social work field practicum students. *International Social Work, 48,* 834-841.

Sindlinger, J. (2011). *Doctoral students experience with using the reflecting team model of supervision online.* (Duquesne University). ProQuest Dissertations and Theses, http://search.proquest.com/docview/885366427?accountid=13901

Wilmshurst, L. (2011). *Child and adolescent psychopathology: A casebook.* Thousand Oaks, CA: Sage.

Contributing Author(s): Dr. Jodi Sindlinger earned her doctorate in Counselor Education and Supervision from Duquesne University. She is an experienced group counselor and instructor of group counseling techniques. Her scholarly interests include using innovative approaches in teacher and counselor preparation and supervising clinical experiences for school counselors.

Dr. Lauren Paulson earned her doctorate in Counselor Education and Supervision from Duquesne University and currently is a Assistant Professor at Allegheny College. She has 13 years of experience in clinical work providing both individual and group counseling, and 4 years of experience teaching at both the undergraduate and graduate level, including group counseling. Her scholarly interests include issues related to rural mental health, counselor education and supervision, and eating disorders.

ACTIVITIES for HUMAN DEVELOPMENT

Chapter 27

The People in Your Neighborhood: Using Community Interviews in a Distance Education Human Development Course

Lacey Ricks, Todd K. Prater, and Amanda M. Evans

Goals and Learning Objectives: The activity has three main goals that align with the Council for the Accreditation for Counseling and Related Educational Programs (CACREP) 2009 standards:
1. To help students describe counseling interventions appropriate during childhood, adolescence, early adulthood, middle and late adulthood stages of life (CACREP II.K.3.a; CACREP II.K.2.c; CACREP CC 2.4; CACREP SC C.2.d).
2. To help students understand and discuss theories of individual and family development and transition across the lifespan. (CACREP II.G.3.a).
3. To help students describe and discuss typical and atypical age related transitions of infancy, childhood, adolescence, early adulthood, middle, and late adulthood (CACREP II.K.3.a; CACREP CC 2.4; CACREP II.G.3.f).

Appropriate Course(s): This specific assignment was developed primarily for a masters-level human development counseling course. The activity could be modified for other counseling classes (i.e., counseling skills, marriage and family therapy, counseling children and adolescents); however, this specific activity will concentrate on human development and the lifespan.

Point in Group When Activity is Used: The premise of this activity is to assign small groups of students to interview volunteers throughout the lifespan. Due to this, the activity should be assigned and discussed at the beginning of the semester with each interview being presented after the instructor has discussed the material on the stage of the lifespan. For example, an interview of someone in older adulthood would be presented toward the end of the semester if the course is presented in chronological order. Specifically for this chapter, we will focus on small groups of four students who will work together to recruit, interview and record four volunteer interviewees across the lifespan (adolescence, young adulthood, middle adulthood and older adulthood). Using the interview questions provided students will interview volunteers in a standardized format so there is consistency amongst the interviews. Once all four interviews are recorded, the small group can work together by communicating through email, message boards or instant messenger and develop a reflective paper on the activity. For this paper, students can incorporate their impressions of the interviewee, the process of working together toward a common goal and the most prevalent human development theories presented in the volunteer interviewee. After the completion of the initial phase of this activity, the recorded videos will be uploaded and included in the class curriculum to initiate class discussions.

Class discussion and viewing of the videos should be distributed intermittently throughout the semester to correlate the videos of varying stages of human development with the syllabus and class timeline. It is important that video viewing and discussion of the content is not completed until the course content on the corresponding human development stage has been completed. Completion of course material before beginning the class discussion is important for ensuring that students have ample knowledge of the material for application in the class discussion (Brindley, Walti, & Blaschke, 2009).

Estimated Time Length: Groups should be notified at the beginning of the semester about this assignment and should be subsequently assigned their small groups. The length of this activity may vary depending on the number of repetitions. Each repetition should take approximately 20 minutes for the small groups to digitally record an interview with a volunteer. Since students are collaborating online to complete their projects, additional time may be needed to complete the project than would otherwise be needed in a traditional class setting (Brindley, Walti, & Blaschke, 2009; Scherling, 2011).

For the large group discussion, several videos of the different small-groups interviews should be uploaded for students to view at their convenience and the Discussion/Process Questions should be distributed (1 to 2 weeks). The counselor educator should identify deadlines and the videos should be watched before transitioning to a class discussion. When initiating a class discussion, the counselor educator should be mindful of the unique needs of distance education students and initiate a flexible large group discussion format. It is recommended that educators consider using message boards to post the Discussion/Process Questions because they allow students to post their thoughts - despite various scheduling needs.

Technology and/or Materials Needed: To complete the activity, students will need access to a digital recording device and access to video conferencing. Each small group will be asked to digitally record their interviews and upload them to the counselor educator. While different devices could be used to record the interviews, it will be important for the counselor educator to identify the type of video file to be uploaded (e.g., files with the extension .wmv). Also, it might be suggested students consider video editing software.

Directions for Activity: To complete this activity, the class should be first divided into small groups of approximately four and will be required to work together to identify and interview four volunteers for this project. All small-groups will be provided the Interview Questionnaire to use with their volunteers. All volunteers must be informed of the purpose of the interview and written consent should be obtained prior to recording the interview. Digitally recorded videos should be 15 to 20 minutes in length. Once all four videos have been recorded, students should upload the video for the small group and counselor educator to view. The counselor educator will review and approve all videos before posting for class discussion. Once the counselor educator approves the video, the video will be uploaded to the class learning systems' video conferencing feature. Through the video conferencing feature, the entire class will review the video and discuss how the volunteer's answers to the pre-identified interview questions correlate with their stages of human development. The counselor educator should help facilitate class discussion on the video through the pre-identified Discussion/Process Questions. The class should use this time to collaborate and discuss the volunteer evolution through the levels of human development and should describe effective counseling interventions that may be used with the volunteers.

<u>Interview Questions</u>

A set of standard interview questions should be used by every student for all volunteer interviewees. The following list is provided as an example and is not exhaustive. Whatever questions are used, students should not modify the questions unless permitted by the course instructor.

Biological/Behavioral
1. Based on your recollection, did you progress through the developmental stages on time (i.e., walking, talking, et cetera)?
2. What is your opinion of how you became you? Were you born this way or are you a product of your environment?
3. What was your relationship like with your family as a child? What is your relationship with your family now?
4. Tell me about a significant event that has occurred in your life. What makes that event stand out to you? Are there any more significant events that stand out in your mind?

Cognitive
1. What was school like for you? Did you find learning to come easy to you or was learning more challenging?
2. How do you prefer to learn now? (i.e., audio, visual, kinesthetic, et cetera).
3. How do you make decisions in life?
4. Tell me about a time when you handled a frustration well. Now, tell me about a time you did not handle a frustration well.
5. If you were comparing yourself to others your age, how would you rate yourself?

Emotional
1. Who do you consider to be the most important people in your life? Can you describe your relationship with them?
2. How would describe your relationship with others? With yourself?
3. How would you describe yourself to others?
4. How have you responded to a relationship that has ended?
5. Are you comfortable with your emotions? What emotion are you comfortable with? What emotions are you not comfortable with?

Discussion/Processing Questions: The Discussion/Process Questions should be used by the counselor educator in a large group discussion.
1. What was your initial impression of the interviewee?
2. If you were working with this volunteer in a clinical setting, how would you utilize the knowledge gleaned from this interview?
3. Based on your developing knowledge of human development theories, was the interviewees content consistent or inconsistent with the content covered in class?
4. What additional information would you like to know about this volunteer?
5. How do you conceptualize the client from a biological, cognitive and/or emotional context?
6. Did the volunteer physically appear to be his/her stated age? Did he/she look older or younger?
7. Did the volunteer cognitively appear to be his/her stated age? Did he/she seem older or younger?
8. Did the volunteer emotionally appear to be his/her stated age? Did he/she seem older or younger?

Potential Adaptations: Accommodations for persons with disabilities should already be achieved through the implementation of a persons with disability university policy and in the course syllabus. However, counselor educators should check with their university policies and procedures to ensure that the distance education class is consistent with the college/university standards. This particular activity does not appear to require adaptions in its current form.

Cautions/Potential Issues: There are several potential issues the counselor educator needs to consider. First, the development of a *Consent to Tape* document is advised that is consistent with the university's standards. Secondly, counselor educators should communicate with students how the interview recordings will be destroyed at the end of the semester and should recommend students delete their recorded copies. Finally, a potential issue with all distance education courses is ensuring all students have access to the technology needed to satisfactorily complete the course. With this particular activity, the counselor educator should verify students have access to a digital recording device.

Credits/References:

Brindley, J. E.,Walti, C., & Blaschke, L. M. (2009).Creating effective learning groups in an online environment. *International Review of Research in Open and Distance Learning, 10* (3), 1-18.

Council for the Accreditation of Counseling and Related Educational Programs. (2009). *Accreditation manual and application.* Alexandria, VA: Author.

Scherling, S. E. (2011). Designing and fostering effective online group projects. *Adult Learning, 22(2),* 13-18.

Contributing Author(s):

Lacey Ricks, EdS, is a graduate student at the Center for Disability Research and Services at Auburn University, completing her Ph.D. in Counseling Education and Supervision. She has five years of experience working as a school counselor. She has individually facilitated and co-facilitated groups with at-risks students. She has a strong interest in working with identified at-risk youth and youth with disabilities.

Todd K. Prater, MSE, MS is the director of the *SOURCE* Center at LaGrange College. The department assists students in creating relationships with alumni and friends of the college who are willing to serve as mentors to help students reach their career aspirations. Todd has facilitated and co-facilitated career guidance groups, substance abuse groups, and disability support groups. He is currently working on a Ph.D. in Counseling Education and Supervision at Auburn University.

Dr. Amanda Evans is an assistant professor of Counselor Education and coordinator of the Clinical Mental Health Counseling master's program at Auburn University. Her research interests include problematic counseling students, counseling men, and ethical decision making.

Chapter 28

The Life of Bambi

Theresa A. Coogan and Victoria L. Bacon

Goals and Learning Objectives:

1. Apply normative development theories and concepts
2. Enhance and strengthen critical thinking skills
3. Collaborate with peers to provide feedback and additional viewpoints

Appropriate Course(s): Human Growth and Development

Point in Group When Activity is Used: Designed to be offered in the middle or latter part of the course when students have had adequate time to develop a working knowledge of developmental theories before beginning this activity.

Estimated Time Length: The assignment is conducted online over the course of one week.

Technology and/or Materials Needed: A Course Management System for the class (e.g., Blackboard) using a class discussion board format, and access to the film *Bambi* (Walt Disney, 1942) is required as well. The use of an online Discussion Board forum (e.g., Blackboard) for this exercise is recommended as it allows for individual posts and peer interaction in a secure online domain.

Directions for Activity: This assignment is conducted online over the course of one week. The theoretical concepts to be applied were acquired via readings, lecture, and discussion the first half of the semester. Students will view the film *Bambi* on their own time in preparation for this week of class.

Post One due by Friday

Select one age appropriate developmental task demonstrated by Bambi or one thing that either Bambi's mother/father did or another character, that served to foster/facilitate normative development for Bambi. Briefly explain the scene and then apply concepts from two theories reviewed in the textbook. The purpose of this assignment is to demonstrate acquired knowledge and the ability to apply the theories and of concepts read and reviewed in the previous weeks.

Post Two due by Sunday

Respond to a minimum of two posts from your peers. For each reply post, please identify a well written idea presented in post one; what make it stand out for you? Next, write a paragraph that expands upon the writing provided by the original author; that is, providing another theoretical lens.

Discussion/Processing Questions:

1. As a counselor-in-training, what are some of the specific ways that you effectively assessed psychological development?
2. In what ways did you effectively apply developmental concepts/theories?
3. In what ways did you provide your peers with constructive feedback?
4. What have you learned as a result of the online discussion with this assignment?

Potential Adaptations: If typing to enter original and reply posts are challenging for the student, another peer, the instructor, or an aid from a Disabilities Office on campus can assist the student to type their reply into a word document that can be copied and pasted easily into the forum within the Discussion Board.

Cautions/Potential Issues: In the in-person class meeting the week before this online exercise, it has been helpful to present and discuss good examples of writing that also infuse and demonstrate higher levels of critical thinking as well as application of theoretical knowledge at the graduate level. This same discussion of examples can be held online if the entire course is offered in a distance education format. During this class meeting (online or in person), encourage students to identify elements that make the examples presented noteworthy. When possible, use examples of writing from students in past semesters. It is also helpful during the week following the activity to highlight and discuss good examples of writing provided by their peers during this exercise.

It has been helpful to also include the directions in the forum when it is created by the instructor. When using Blackboard or another Course Management System, remind students about creating string threads (e.g., several reply posts connected to each other). Students can re-name the subject line in their post to assist with organizing the content. When there are string threads, students are encouraged to use the "collect" function through Blackboard so that they can view all replies at one time.

Inform students they will need to obtain and watch the movie on their own time. Recommend public libraries as places to obtain the video at little or no cost. They may need to plan ahead to obtain the video depending on the size of the class and the number of libraries in the local area. Students may also choose to organize a group showing of the movie on their own time in preparation for the class.

Credits/References:

Film: *Bambi*. Walt Disney (Producer). David D. Hand (Director). (1942). *Bambi* [Animated Film]. United States: RKO Radio Pictures.

Contributing Author(s): Dr. Theresa A. Coogan is an Assistant Professor in the Department of Counselor Education at Bridgewater State University, and teaches general counseling and school counseling courses. She is an active member in ASGW and has an active research agenda exploring group work skills and techniques to enhance learning for counseling students.

Dr. Victoria L. Bacon is a Professor in the Department of Counselor Education at Bridgewater State University and the primary instructor for all group courses. She is an active member in ASGW and has several presentations and publications on group work. She also recently served on the Editorial Board for the Journal of Specialists in Group Work.

ACTIVITIES for HELPING RELATIONSHIPS

Chapter 29

Visualizing Our Purpose

Kylie P. Dotson-Blake

Goals and Learning Objectives:

1. To give voice to each group member's expectations of the purpose of the group
2. To help develop a cohesive, clear purpose for the group with the investment and support of group members.

Appropriate Course(s): Appropriate for all courses based on image used and focus of the discussion.

Point in Group When Activity is Used: Can be used at anytime with the understanding that level of disclosure and depth of conversation will be impacted. Best used after a certain level of trust and cohesion has been created to increase level of disclosure and safety involved among members.

Estimated Time Length: This activity can be conducted synchronously or asynchronously. If conducted synchronously, allow 15 to 30 minutes for completion and processing. If conducted asynchronously, allow the discussion to remain open for a few days to allow all members to participate in the development, discussion and processing.

Technology and/or Materials Needed:

- VoiceThread (Available at http://voicethread.com)

- Phone, Web Cam, or Internal Computer Microphone (Text Entry can be substituted)

The purpose of using VoiceThread is to allow group members to participate in an asynchronous discussion. Here is an example of what your VoiceThread may look like.

As librarians we feel the need to provide appropriate and meaningful services to all students, however, we may be challenged by the lack of information, training and access to crucial services and student records. Counselors also feel the need to provide appropriate and meaningful services to all students; however, they may be challenged as to knowledge of resources, technical skills, and means to provide resources to all students. This presents an opportunity for these two significant departments in schools to work together to strengthen each other. Consider what you do and what you know. Think also of what you perceive school counselors to be responsible for. Can you envision ways to support each other in serving the students that you teach?

School Counselor & School Librarian Working Together = Success for Students!!

Many other websites and products could be used for this purpose, including BlackBoard, Moodle, Tangler, etc.

Directions for Activity: This activity begins by having the instructor choose an image to share with the group. This image can be anything that the instructor feels is interesting and will spark discussion among members. The image will serve as the focal point of a discussion of group members' expectations about the purpose of the group.

After choosing the image, the group leader should post the image on VoiceThread with the prompt, *"Post a comment relating this picture to your expectations of the purpose of our group,"* and open the discussion.

Welcome group members. During this session, we will be working to clarify our expectations and hopes about the purpose of our group. This discussion will be conducted asynchronously allowing you to jump in and share your thoughts. We will be conducting this discussion using VoiceThread.com. Please click on the link I have sent to you below. (Invitation can be generated and sent directly from VoiceThread.com). As group members post comments, please read and respond to the comments, just as you would in a face-to-face group session, allowing us to have a rich discussion of the purpose of our group.

Once group members start responding to the image, the instructor should jump in and make comments about posts as well.

Here is an example to view: http://voicethread.com/share/2182493

Discussion/Processing Questions:

1. When you viewed the image, what were your initial reactions about possible links between the image and our group's purpose?
2. What characteristics of the image serve as a metaphor for the process we might experience coming together as a group?
3. How might you modify the image to more directly align with what you believe to be the purpose of our group?
4. Examples of image-specific processing questions using the Tarpon Image that was included in the sample VoiceThread:
   a. How might the process of stretching our minds and thoughts about potential links between a picture of a tarpon and our counseling group, be similar to our process for engaging with each other around topics of discussion in group?
   b. A tarpon is a fish that is amazingly comfortable with aeronautical acrobatics. These fish use the process of jumping to great heights out of the water to "throw the hook" and escape when snagged by an angler. How does this fish know that jumping into an unfamiliar environment (the air as opposed to the water) will open the doors to freedom? How does this process mirror our group's beginning and purpose?

Potential Adaptations: The group leader can adapt this activity in a number of ways, including:

1. Allow members to choose an image and post it with an explanation of how it relates to the group's purpose.
2. Post a video, song or other form of media rather than image as the prompt for discussion.

Cautions/Potential Issues: Group members will need to develop an account with VoiceThread.com. These accounts are free and many helpful tools are offered to facilitate the use of VoiceThread.com. Since comments can be posted using webcams, internal computer microphones, by text/typing or by phone there should be no barriers to all members participating easily and without additional fees or costs. Group members should be aware that if the instructor is not using a professional level account (requires a fee) there is limited security so it would be best to not share highly sensitive information, including full names and identification information in order to ensure confidentiality of discussions. Addressing confidentiality with respect to groups would be appropriate to remind students the class expectations about keeping learned information about each other private.

Contributing Author(s): Dr. Kylie P. Dotson-Blake is an Assistant Professor in the Department of Higher, Adult and Counselor Education at East Carolina University. As a school counselor and as a family counselor, she has conducted groups with young children, adolescents, and adults. Her research focuses on cultural identity development and the impact of culture and race on family-school-community partnership engagement.

Chapter 30

Demonstrating the Core Conditions of Counseling

Kimberly A. Donovan and Daniel J. Weigel

Goals and Learning Objectives:
1. To decrease anxiety and foster group cohesion as early in the course as possible through the use of nonthreatening role plays
2. To help students better understand and implement the core conditions of the counseling relationship – empathy, unconditional positive regard, and genuineness
3. To experience potential strengths and limitations of online counseling and online supervision.

Appropriate Course(s): Helping Relationships, specifically a counseling Pre-Practicum or other introductory clinical skills course (in which students are learning the basic relationship-building skills and the core conditions of counseling)

Point in Group When Activity is Used: Early in the class – the second class period in a regular 15-week schedule OR the first class period in a shorter 8-week course, after the core conditions have been discussed.

Estimated Time Length: 1 hour-1.5 hours (can be shorter or longer depending on class size and processing time allowed)

Technology and/or Materials Needed: This activity may be performed via webcam or discussion board via Blackboard, for example.

Purpose of Technology

Any software that allows real-time discussion and/or live video feed is preferable, so that students may simulate counseling sessions. A web-conferencing program, such as WebEx, could be utilized. Students could record these activities and then upload them to a secure server, such as voicethread.com, for the course instructor and observer in the triad to offer feedback/provide supervision and insights and for the entire class to observe and process.

Directions for Activity: After forming triads, each student chooses a role to play. The instructor does not share the objective of each activity with the students until during the process portion of the activity. The students do not share their assigned scripts with the other members of the triad until the end of each activity. In order that all students may experience the role of counselor, client, and observer, the students switch roles for each activity after processing their experiences using the questions at the end of these instructions.

1. **EMPATHY:**
   A. *Empathy Role–Play #1.* Objective: To demonstrate inaccurate empathy.

   Directions for Client: You are a client who has been to several counselors in the past and have been generally dissatisfied with your experiences to this point. With previous counselors you have not felt listened to and left their offices feeling unimportant and dissatisfied with your counseling experiences.

   Your doctor has recently been insistent that you should see a counselor regarding your struggles with your temper and with panic attacks. Your job is to sit down with this new counselor and attempt to explain to him your situation, and specifically your hesitancy to try counseling again. You are subtly and not so subtly seeking reassurance from your counselor that s/he will listen to you and give you her/his undivided attention.

   <u>Directions for Counselor</u>: You are a counselor who is very distracted by things going on in your personal life. Unfortunately, you are not able to set your personal life aside during the session. Therefore, during this session, you will intentionally reflect back inaccurately what your client is saying. Miss the boat. Offer immediate solutions and advice without listening to what your client is saying. This advice will obviously be inappropriate, since you are not listening to what your client is saying. You are very distracted during the whole session.

   Directions for Observer: Carefully watch the session and share reactions and insights at the end of the process.

   INSTRUCTOR: Process the role-play with counselor, client, observer, of each triad and then with the class using the questions at the end of this activity.

   B. *Empathy Role–Play #2.* Objective: To demonstrate accurate empathy.

   Directions for Client: Share a problem or issue with the counselor. This should <u>NOT</u> be a real issue. Please role-play a problem or an issue in order to protect your privacy online.

   Directions for Counselor: As the client shares the story, reflect back what you are hearing. This is a *process* activity, meaning that reflections should occur during the activity, as well as in a summary at the end of the practice session. Do not use questions during this exercise. Demonstrate accurate empathy using brief paraphrases and feeling reflections.

   Directions for Observer: Take notes regarding counselor observations during the session. At the end of the session, you will provide feedback to the counselor regarding the reflections made in the session. What did the counselor do well? In what areas might the counselor improve? Did the counselor ask questions?

INSTRUCTOR: Process the role-play with counselor, client, observer, of each triad and then with the class using the questions at the end of this activity.

2. **UNCONDITIONAL POSITIVE REGARD:**
   A. ***Unconditional Positive Regard Role-Play #1.*** Objective: To demonstrate a lack of positive regard.

   Directions for Client: You are an adolescent who is very proud of the number of tattoos and body piercings that you have. You are very willing to talk about the pride you have in having all of these tattoos and piercings. Talk about how important these tattoos and piercings are to you and your self-identity. Also, talk about how much your parents disapprove of who you've become. You are thinking about running away from home.

   Directions for Counselor: You have a child who has recently gotten a tattoo and you are furious. You can barely sleep at night thinking about the tattoo and your rebellious child. Not surprisingly, you end up with an adolescent client who loves to talk about his/her tattoos and other eccentricities. As much as you try, you can't help but pass judgment on this client. The judgment comes forth through your reflections both subtly and blatantly. Eventually you end up giving some advice to your client.

   Directions for Observer: Carefully watch the session and share reactions and insights at the end of the process. Provide feedback to the counselor regarding the ways his/her judgment did or did not show up in the session.

   INSTRUCTOR: Process the role-play with counselor, client, observer, of each triad and then with the class using the questions at the end of this activity.
   B. ***Unconditional Positive Regard Role-Play #2.*** Objective: To listen without judgment.

   Directions for Client: You share with your counselor that you are required to come to her/him because you were recently caught driving while under the influence of marijuana. You see nothing wrong with smoking pot. After all, it is legal in many countries. It's even prescribed by doctors in several states! You are very clear in stating that you think it's a joke to have to come to counseling and do not plan on changing your behavior.

   Directions for the counselor: Your job is to reflect back nonjudgmentally what you are hearing in the counseling session. It is your job to decide what this will look like, but you are not permitted to pass judgment on your client through your reactions and nonverbal/verbal communications (using minimal encouragers, paraphrases, and feeling reflections).

    Directions for Observer: Carefully watch the session and share reactions and insights at the end of the process. Provide feedback to the counselor regarding the ways his/her judgment did or did not show up in the session.

    INSTRUCTOR: Process the role-play with counselor, client, observer, of each triad and then with the class using the questions at the end of this activity.

3. **GENUINENESS:**
   A. *Genuineness Role-Play #1.* Objective: To demonstrate a lack of genuineness.

    Directions for Client: You share with your counselor how hard graduate school is for you. You are clearly the victim of a conspiracy and assert that you simply cannot believe how much homework and papers "they" pile on. You whine and complain incessantly about how there is simply *no way you can ever get it done.* You are convinced that you are going to fail and that's exactly what "they" want. Your job in this role-play is to be as annoying as you possibly can (e.g., touch everything, rotate around in your chair, comment on your counselor's weird shoes, etc.) as you share your story.

    Directions for Counselor: If there's one thing you can't stand, it's a client who whines all the time and never changes anything. Unfortunately for you, that's exactly what this client does. Quite frankly, you are fed up with whining clients, but have decided you're not going to say anything about it. Therefore, everything that comes out of your mouth is supportive for the client. Unfortunately, you can't hide your nonverbal communications. Therefore, everything you say with your body indicates that you cannot stand this client (e.g., rolling your eyes when the client isn't looking, sighing, showing disinterest, etc).

    Directions for Observer: Carefully watch the session and share reactions and insights at the end of the process. Provide feedback to the counselor regarding the ways he or she did (or did not) demonstrate genuineness in the session.

    INSTRUCTOR: Process the role-play with counselor, client, observer, of each triad and then with the class using the questions at the end of this activity.

   B. *Genuineness Role-Play #2.* Objective: To practice reflections with genuineness.

    Directions for Client: Complete one of the following open-ended statements and share your feelings with your counselor in session:
~ When I'm doing an exercise like this in class, I…
~ Regarding this class, I am nervous about…

~ One of my biggest fears right now is...

~ Toward you right now, I feel...

Directions for Counselor: Reflect back to the client (in your own words) exactly what you hear the client say.

Directions for Observer: Carefully watch the experience and share reactions and insights at the end of the process. Provide feedback to the counselor regarding the ways he or she did (or did not) demonstrate genuineness in the session.

INSTRUCTOR: Process the role-play with counselor, client, observer, of each triad and then with the class using the questions at the end of this activity.

Discussion/Processing Questions: These questions should be asked as part of a large group discussion at the end of each role-play.

1. What is it like to have things reflected back to you in a different way from what you are used to (counselor not asking questions and reflecting instead)?

2. What is it like to be client when your counselor does not have empathy? Is judgmental? Is not genuine? What is it like to be client when your counselor demonstrates empathy? Unconditional positive regard? Genuineness?

3. What is it like to be counselor when demonstrating/not demonstrating these conditions? Are you comfortable demonstrating these conditions as a counselor? Explain.

Potential Adaptations: No particular adaptations should be needed to accommodate individuals with disabilities aside from basic ADA requirements in designing a web-based course. As long as the learner has a website or document "reader" software client, this activity would be very appropriate for those living with disabilities.

Cautions/Potential Issues: In order to avoid unnecessary anxiety, harm, and potential invasion of privacy online, the instructor must instruct students at the onset of the activity and remind them throughout the activity that the role-plays are not each other's real-life issues.

Contributing Author(s): Kimberly A. Donovan, Ph.D., NCC, LPC, ACS is an associate professor of Counseling and Program Coordinator of the Master of Arts Degree Program in Clinical Mental Health Counseling at Southeastern Oklahoma State University in Durant, Oklahoma. Dr. Donovan is a counselor educator and Licensed Professional Counselor with experience providing individual and group counseling to children, adolescents, and adults with a multitude of issues in a variety of settings. As a counselor educator, she has received extensive clinical supervision training and has over a decade of experience providing clinical supervision to counselors-in-training. Dr.

Donovan's research and professional interests include clinical supervision, counselor training and professional identity development issues, eating disorders, bullying prevention, and domestic violence awareness and prevention.

Dr. Daniel J. Weigel is a professor of Counseling and Coordinator of Clinical Experiences in the Master of Arts Degree Program in Clinical Mental Health Counseling at Southeastern Oklahoma State University in Durant, Oklahoma. Dr. Weigel is a counselor educator and Licensed Professional Counselor who has extensive experience providing individual and group counseling in both inpatient and outpatient settings, specifically to individuals suffering from substance use and co-occurring disorders. He has taught, consulted, presented, and published on a wide variety of counseling training issues over the past 14 years working as a counselor educator. His research interests include prescription medication abuse, substance dependence issues, psychopharmacology, ethical issues pertaining to rural mental health counseling, and clinical supervision.

Author Index

The Association for Specialists in Group Work (ASGW)

What is ASGW?

The Association for Specialists in Group Work was founded in 1973.

The purposes of ASGW are to:
• Establish standards for professional and ethical group practice.
• Support research and the dissemination of knowledge related to group work.
• Provide leadership and training in group specialties.

In addition, ASGW seeks to extend counseling, consulting, and organizational development through group process, to build community through group work, to provide a forum for examining innovative and developing concepts in group work, to foster diversity and dignity in our groups, and to be a model of effective group practice.

Who Joins ASGW?

Members include counselors and other professionals who are interested in and specialize in group work, and who value the creation of community and the provision of group service to members, their clients, and the profession of counseling. Membership is for persons who use group leadership as a process to facilitate the growth and development of people. Applications include mental health agencies, schools, community organizations, colleges and hospitals. To learn more about ASGW, go to www.asgw.org.

Benefits of Joining ASGW

• *Journal for Specialists in Group Work*, a quarterly journal that publishes research and practical and innovative articles of relevance to group practitioners.
• The *Group Worker*, a newsletter published three times annually, providing regional and naional news related to group work, legislative updates, and special articles of interest to group practitioners.

• Participation at member rates for ASGW group training events conducted in regional areas across the country. ASGW workshop coordinators work with local sponsors to offer a variety of group training workshops that provide attractive opportunities for continued professional development.
• Local support through state and regional organizations for specialists in group work.

Types of Membership

ASGW membership categories include Professional, Regular, New Professional, Student, and Retired. ACA membership is not required for membership in ASGW.

Professional: Professional members hold a graduate degree in counseling or a closely related field and are engaged in the teaching, practice or research of group work. Professional members have all rights and benefits of membership in ASGW.
Regular: Regular members are members who have an interest in group work, including related professional groups such as social work, psychology, and counselors from countries other than the United States. Regular members have all rights and benefits of membership in ASGW, except holding elective office.
New Professional: A New Professional is someone who has graduated with a masters or a doctorate within the past 12 months. Status is good for one year.
Student: Student members are persons who are actively enrolled in a graduate program and studying group work. Student members have all rights and benefits of membership in ASGW, except holding elective office.
Retired: Members who are retired from the counseling profession and have been active ACA and ASGW member for the past 5 consecutive years.

Division Processing Fee

To join ASGW without joining ACA, a processing fee of $10 will apply.

Become a Member of ASGW Today!

ASGW/ACA Membership Dues
(valid thru 6/30/2013)

ASGW subscribes to and operates under the auspices of the ACA (American Counseling Association) Code of Ethics. By becoming an ASGW member, you are agreeing to be subject to the rules, regulations, and enforcement of the terms of the ACA Code of Ethics, which include appropriate sanctions up to suspension or expulsion from ACA and public notice about any such action. The ACA Code of Ethics of available at www.counseling.org or www.asgw.org

Choose one	ASGW		ACA		Total
Professional	$40.00	+	$163.00	=	$203.00
Regular	$40.00	+	$163.00	=	$203.00
New Professional **	$27.00	+	$93.00	=	$120.00
Student*	$27.00	+	$93.00	=	$120.00
Retired	$27.00	+	$93.00	=	$120.00
Joining ASGW only	**ASGW**		**Processing Fee**		**Total**
Professional	$40.00	+	$10.00	=	$50.00
Regular	$40.00	+	$10.00	=	$50.00
New Professional **	$27.00	+	$10.00	=	$37.00
Student*	$27.00	+	$10.00	=	$37.00
Retired	$27.00	+	$10.00	=	$37.00

Adding ASGW to ACA Membership **(For current ACA members only)** If adding ASGW to a current ACA membership, call Member Services at 800-347-6647 x 222 for prorated dues amount to coordinate with your ACA renewal date.					
Professional ASGW	$40.00		New Professional ASGW	=	$27.00
Student ASGW	$27.00		Retired ASGW	=	$27.00

Join on the Web!
http://www.counseling.org/Counselors/MemberJoin.asp

Join by Phone! 1-800-347-6647

Group Counseling Activities for Online Learning